Dos
&
Don'ts
of
EDUCATION
REFORM

Studies in the Postmodern Theory of Education

Joe L. Kincheloe and Shirley R. Steinberg
General Editors

Vol. 283

PETER LANG
New York • Washington, D.C./Baltimore • Bern
Frankfurt am Main • Berlin • Brussels • Vienna • Oxford

Anthony M. Roselli

Dos
&
Don'ts

of

EDUCATION

REFORM

*Toward a Radical Remedy
for Educational Failure*

PETER LANG
New York • Washington, D.C./Baltimore • Bern
Frankfurt am Main • Berlin • Brussels • Vienna • Oxford

Library of Congress Cataloging-in-Publication Data

Roselli, Anthony M.
Dos and don'ts of education reform: toward a radical remedy
for educational failure / Anthony M. Roselli.
p. cm. — (Counterpoints; v. 283)
Includes bibliographical references and index.
1. Educational planning—United States. 2. Education—United States—
Evaluation. 3. Education—Social aspects—United States.
4. School improvement programs—United States. I. Title.
II. Series: Counterpoints (New York, N.Y.); v. 283.
LC89.R67   379.73—dc22   2004001632
ISBN 978-0-8204-7260-7
ISSN 1058-1634

Bibliographic information published by **Die Deutsche Bibliothek**
Die Deutsche Bibliothek lists this publication in the "Deutsche
Nationalbibliografie"; detailed bibliographic data is available
on the Internet at http://dnb.ddb.de/.

Cover design by Joni Holst

The paper in this book meets the guidelines for permanence and durability
of the Committee on Production Guidelines for Book Longevity
of the Council of Library Resources.

© 2005, 2013 Peter Lang Publishing, Inc., New York
29 Broadway, 18th floor, New York, NY 10006
www.peterlang.com

All rights reserved.
Reprint or reproduction, even partially, in all forms such as microfilm,
xerography, microfiche, microcard, and offset strictly prohibited.

Printed in the United States of America

OFFERED AS A GIFT OF LOVE
to my wife, Patricia, and to my children—
Alison, Melissa, and Matthew . . .
and also to the memory of my mother and father

CONTENTS

ACKNOWLEDGMENTS ix

INTRODUCTION 1

PART I | THE FORGOTTEN MEANING OF REFORM

CHAPTER 1
REFORM EFFORTS ACROSS THE NATION: A SYNTHESIS   7

CHAPTER 2
A CLOSE LOOK AT REFORM IN ONE STATE:
THE MASSACHUSETTS EXPERIMENT   23

CHAPTER 3
RESULTS REDUCED TO NUMBERS:
THE RACE TO SHOW ACHIEVEMENT GAINS   41

CHAPTER 4
SEMANTICS OF EDUCATION REFORM:
WORDS AND CONCEPTS DEVOID OF MEANING   55

PART II | CURRICULUM, INSTRUCTION, AND ASSESSMENT: THREE ESSENTIALS LOST IN POLITICAL AND HEGEMONIC MANEUVERING

CHAPTER 5
CURRICULUM AS KNOWLEDGE:
PUBLIC VS. PRIVATE SIGNIFICANCE   73

CHAPTER 6
INSTRUCTION AS THEORY: THE WIDE GAP
BETWEEN TALKING AND WALKING   87

CHAPTER 7
ASSESSMENT AS NONSENSE: WHEN ART
TRIES TO DOUBLE AS SCIENCE   103

**PART III | DECIPHERING THE JARGON:
CALLING UPON GOOD SENSE AND PRAGMATISM**

CHAPTER 8
A CULTURAL STUDY OF SUCCESS   123

CHAPTER 9
FROM PANACEAS TO MULTIPLE PERSPECTIVES
AND PRUDENT USE OF REINVENTION   135

CONCLUSION   147

REFERENCES   151

INDEX   157

ACKNOWLEDGMENTS

THIS BOOK IS THE RESULT of many years of thinking about, and practicing, education in a variety of school settings. Along the way, many friends and colleagues knowingly and unwittingly challenged my ideas, compelling me to dig even more deeply into the data, the research, and the knowledge base. I am grateful for their inspiring words and straightforward talk on all matters which relate to the improvement of society, of schools, and of the lives of children.

I want to mention especially the following people who gave me reasons to continue my scholarly work: Edward Korza, George DeGeorge, Henry Giroux, Pamela Halpern, Sylvie Pressman, Charles DePascale, Joan Winchester Sachs, Mary Forte Hayes, Jeffrey Young, Judy Collins, Manuela Bartiromo, Joseph FitzGerald, Rena Mirkin, Brenda Brown, Noreen Burdett, Ray Harper, Paula Girouard McCann, Douglas Sears, Sandra Guryan, Tina Sullivan, Frank Giuliano, Roseanne Mulherin, Laura Coyle, Allen Adams, and Mary Schofield.

Finally, my sincere thanks to the talented publishing team at Peter Lang: Phyllis Korper, Senior Acquisitions Editor; Lisa Dillon, Production and Creative Director; Joe Kincheloe and Shirley Steinberg, Series Editors; and Christopher Myers, Managing Director.

INTRODUCTION

I WOULD RATHER WRITE A BOOK on how to improve, simply, upon the learning outcomes of schooling. Schooling in America, I mean to say. But that luxury is not available in this era of mismatched priorities, where society wants schools to solve societal problems while schools can barely keep up with the curricular changes necessitated by technological advances, by the ever-changing workplace, and by the emphasis on thinking skills valued by colleges and universities. The situation, the status quo, at the beginning of the twenty-first century requires yet another look at the fundamentals of education, forgotten variables in the equation of what contributes truly to excellent educational results. I would rather not be the author (this is my first book) of a piece of writing that demonstrates how to reform education, because schools should be allowed to figure this out for themselves. Yet many still claim that educational failure persists to an extent that warrants systematic reform of the entire schooling enterprise. I do not think that any reform package can accomplish such a homogenized goal in such a diverse, multifaceted array of schools in the United States. Should we even try to do this? Is there ever a reasonable guideline applicable to *all* schools?

The basis for my beginning a book on education reform was precisely the recognition that all other reform efforts have not/are not accomplishing the elusive goal of improving education. Indeed, my own research that began in the summer of 2000 looked at the education reform efforts across all fifty states. Results were uniformly mixed; improvements continue to be difficult to obtain. I had come to the uncomfortable conclusion after my meta-analysis of reform results reported by the states (chapter 1) that nowhere was there a "model" reform effort worthy of replication. I must admit that what

I found did not surprise me based on my close examination of one state's efforts (chapter 2). Most, or all, state-mandated reforms are data driven—that is, are designed to generate test results that are then used to attempt to demonstrate "improvement" upon an ill-defined baseline of achievement existing prior to the start of reform. Accelerated Schools, Core Knowledge approach, Success for All, New American Schools, America's Choice—all of these so-called whole school reforms (to name only the most prolific) have shown mixed results and uneven patterns of "improvement." It is unfortunate that such large investments of time, money, effort, and myriad resources end up accomplishing so little. But we should not be surprised.

Fortunate enough to receive three development grants, I continued to pursue my research on "reform." There is little doubt in my mind that without some support I would have abandoned the project since the labor intensiveness of finding patterns among millions of pieces of data is the kind of endeavor one accomplishes only with assistance. I was lucky enough to have support and encouragement from colleagues, friends, and family. And after all, I do have something to say; no, I have a lifetime of accumulated observation of, and direct experience in, schooling from grades K to 12.

My own cynicism dates back to 1990 when I began to write colloquially on education. I began (but did not finish) a manuscript that, loosely arranged around relevant topics (curriculum, instruction, and so forth), was greeted with some interest by a publisher in California. The title, "Out of Time: Urgent Thoughts on American Education for Parents and Teachers," reflected my disposition at the time that embodied a frustration toward the lack of progress in making schools more responsive to the needs of students and the desires of parents. I thought, at the time, that a focus on teachers and teaching would reveal a viable solution; but I was wrong. It is important to state now that the core sentiments of "Out of Time" remain alive within me. It would not be inaccurate to say that current times warrant, perhaps, a more forceful response to educational failure, if we believe that the failure in schools, and of schools, is a core reason for the decline in our quality of life (if indeed we believe that schools have anything at all to do with life, or quality). In fact, I had intended, ten years ago, to attempt (had I finished and published the first manuscript) a sequel that I would have entitled "One More Chance: Critical Solutions to Urgent Problems in American Education." The sentiment in the sequel would have more closely reflected that found in *Revolutionary Pedagogies: Cultural Politics, Instituting Education, and the Discourse of Theory* (Trifonas, 2000). My current state of mind holds on firmly to the idea of urgency but frames the issue of "school improvement" in a new light, perhaps a bolder and surely a broader one.

Introduction 3

My experience tells me that the same problems exist, exacerbated, in 2004. Since 1990 we have seen a rash of shootings in schools, experienced horrific tragedies in New York City and Washington, D.C., three times gone to war in the Middle East, and declared war on terrorism. Through it all we have bemoaned a gradual loss of the self. The urgency that I noted back in 1990 is much more palpable in 2004. The core problems—schooling in general and curriculum, instruction, and assessment in particular—that existed then are all still with us. The solutions thus far have not proven effective; the reforms have been sporadic and uneven in result. Why do we continue to search for the answers in new programs? Why do we persist in trying to measure results with increasingly ubiquitous testing programs? Are we confident in the validity, reliability, and potential to improve the human condition of our standardized, norm-referenced tests?

My heart tells me that our current direction in reform is ill advised. Have we defined educational problems in a way that engenders confidence and trust? Do we believe that our agenda is supportable and worthy of widespread action? Will everyone (anyone) feel a change in heart (that is, become more compassionate) as a result of successful reform of schooling, whatever that might mean?

My soul intimates that I must reject the false hopes set up and reinforced by loud, prolific reform machines: political speeches, think tanks, and legislated improvement of education. All of these combine to produce, I am saddened to say, a very disingenuous portrayal of both our problems and the recommended solutions. Neither is as bad nor as effectively articulated as the prophets of doom/hope would have us believe. Have there been any honest attempts to help children, all children, succeed in school and in life? Is compassion prevalent in curriculum, instruction, and assessment? Or is the ghost of mediocrity ("A Nation at Risk," 1983) ever-present among education professionals and among those who claim schools as their rightful stomping ground upon which to shower their scantily clad platforms of reform of teaching and learning? In essence, do any one of these voices offer sincere guidelines for how we might help children acquire an esprit de corps based on love, service to others, honest intellectual inquiry, and sound moral living? Have we even cared to ponder such an idea? The empty rhetoric of NCLB (No Child Left Behind) will do nothing to heal our spirit. (The NCLB legislation, a bill passed by the U.S. Congress in 2001, is actually a reauthorization of the ESEA [Elementary and Secondary Education Act], first enacted in 1965.) (See chapter 1 for an analysis of the NCLB legislation.)

I, therefore, have continued to write a manuscript that is an essentialist philosophy of education reform with a notable bent toward phenomenology. This is, though, neither clichéd nor old-fashioned. Rather, this book is a return to ideas that are so much more powerful and more inspiring than the bland, worn-out diatribes of politicians, pedagogues, and pedants. The schoolhouse and the academy cannot tolerate another day of half-reasoned, ill-defined agendas that waste precious time and endanger our children, our future. There have been too many tragedies and too much sorrow: our inaction seems to cause actions we hoped to prevent. It is time for a return to the sound reasoning and morally based notions inherent in the best of curriculum theory, instructional methodology, and authentic assessment.

Why would I possess any solutions to end educational failure? I only know my intention: to search for the remedies that speak to a combination of mind, heart, and soul. And I do this to remind myself that few, if any, mortals can fix the enormous disequilibrium present in our disturbed sense of faith in American schooling. Any solutions that I dare offer in this book will be an attempt to restore educational integrity to the core, essential elements of schooling . . . and of living.

The book is divided into three sections:

Part I **The Forgotten Meaning of Reform** in which I attempt to take an inventory of reform across the fifty states, focus closely on one state (Massachusetts), and make the argument that the debate on reform "got lost" in rhetoric, misuse of language, and an ill-advised testing frenzy.

Part II **Curriculum, Instruction, and Assessment: Three Essentials Lost in Political and Hegemonic Maneuvering** in which I reconnect with what I view as the best of curriculum theory, of research on instruction that is usually ignored, and of the artful nature of assessment. All three of these key elements of schooling offer hope in the debate on reform if we begin to seek the true, intended meanings of these elements.

Part III **Deciphering the Jargon: Calling upon Good Sense and Pragmatism** in which I paint a picture of success based in cultural context, that is, success that is valued in a sociological frame of reference. Not entirely individualistic, success is often a function of group definition. I will suggest a reinvention of what constitutes "legitimate" reform effort and offer a pragmatic perspective on schooling in the twenty-first century.

PART I

THE FORGOTTEN MEANING OF REFORM

CHAPTER 1

REFORM EFFORTS ACROSS THE NATION
A Synthesis

AFTER AN EXTENSIVE META-ANALYSIS of education reform results reported by the fifty states, I have come to the uncomfortable conclusion that there is no model reform effort worthy of replication. My conclusion is based on an extensive analysis of results published by the states through several documents: reports published by the *Education Commission of the States*, in Denver, Colorado; the annual reports entitled "Quality Counts" (1998, 2003), published by *Education Week;* and "Technology Counts" (2003) also published by the Editorial Projects in Education of *Education Week*. I have also made a concerted effort to gather information on education reform through participation at the AERA (American Educational Research Association) and NEERO (New England Educational Research Organization). I have attended conferences at the regional organization since 1991 and the national association (AERA) since 1999. Millions of hours of effort, billions of dollars in expenditure, and innumerable well-intentioned proposals have all combined to yield a paltry picture of educational improvement in the public school system of the United States.

The aforementioned *Education Commission of the States* in Denver, Colorado, recently reported on what is called *The Nation's Report Card:*

Mathematics 2000, published by the National Center for Education Statistics in Washington, D.C. The major findings were as follows:

FOR THE NATION

▌ Fourth-, Eighth-, and Twelfth-grade students had higher average scores in 2000 than in 1990, the first assessment year in which the current mathematics framework was used. Fourth and eighth graders showed steady progress across the decade; twelfth graders made gains from 1990 to 1996, but their average score declined between 1996 and 2000.*

▌ In 2000 the percentage of students performing at or above proficient was 26% at grade 4, 27% at grade 8, and 17% at grade 12. At each grade the percentage of students performing at or above this level was higher in 2000 than in 1990. There were gains over the decade at the basic and advanced levels as well. However, from 1996 to 2000 the percentage of twelfth graders reaching the basic level declined.*

▌ Score increases are evident across the performance distribution—higher-, middle-, and lower-performing students have made gains since 1990 at each grade. At grade 12, however, the decline in the average score between 1996 and 2000 was reflected mostly in the scores of students in the middle- and lower-performance ranges: scores declined only at the 50th, 25th, and 10th percentiles, that is, the scores of students at the higher end of the SES (socioeconomic status) ladder did not decline.*

---

*Executive Summary, The Nation's Report Card: Mathematics 2000.

Author's Note: The 2003 results show increases in grades 4 and 8 in the majority of states. Yet the average percentage scoring in the "proficient" range across all fifty states was: grade 4: 31% and grade 8: 27%. Of even more concern is the fact that the achievement levels themselves (basic, proficient, and advanced), while rigorous, have not been proved valid or reliable (Manzo and Galley, 2003).

FOR THE REGIONS

▌ Average scores in the Southeast, Central, and West were higher in 2000 than in 1990 for students in all three grades. Average scores in the Northeast were higher in 2000 than in 1990 for fourth and eighth graders, but the apparent difference for twelfth graders was not statistically significant.

▌ In 2000 average scores for fourth graders were higher in the Northeast and Central regions than in the Southeast. For eighth and twelfth graders, scores in the Northeast, Central, and West were higher than in the Southeast.

FOR THE STATES AND OTHER JURISDICTIONS

▌ In the NAEP (National Assessment of Educational Progress) 2000 state-by-state assessment, forty states and six other jurisdictions at grade 4 and thirty-nine states and five other jurisdictions at grade 8 met the participation guidelines for reporting results. Only public schools participated in the state-by-state assessment.

AT GRADE 4

▌ In 2000 no state scored higher than these nine: Connecticut, Indiana, Iowa, Kansas, Massachusetts, Minnesota, North Carolina, Texas, and Vermont. The states with the highest percentages of students at or above *proficient* were Connecticut, Indiana, Kansas, Massachusetts, Michigan, Minnesota, and Vermont. Their percentages at or above *proficient* ranged from 29% to 34%.

▌ Of the thirty-six states and jurisdictions that participated in both 2000 and the first state assessment at grade 4 in 1992, twenty-six had higher average scores in 2000 than in 1992.

AT GRADE 8

▌ In 2000 no state scored higher than these three: Kansas, Minnesota, and Montana. The two states with the highest percentages of students at or above *proficient* were Minnesota (40%) and Montana (37%).

▌ Of the thirty-one states and jurisdictions that participated in both 2000 and the first state assessment at grade 8 in 1990, twenty-seven had higher average scores in 2000 than in 1990.

RACE/ETHNICITY

▌ In 2000, at all three grade levels, the average scores of white students were higher than those of black, Hispanic, and American Indian students.

▌ In 2000 at grade 12 the average score of Asian/Pacific Islander students was higher than the scores of white, black, and Hispanic students.

▌ White, black, and Hispanic students at grades 4 and 8 had higher average scores in 2000 than in 1990. At grade 12 only white students had a higher average score in 2000 than in 1990. The score gaps between white students and black students and between white students and Hispanic students were large at every grade. There was no evidence in the 2000 assessment of any narrowing of the racial/ethnic group score gaps since 1990.

PARENTS' LEVEL OF EDUCATION

▌ Generally, students in grades 8 and 12 with higher scores reported higher levels of parental education in 2000. This result is consistent with past NAEP assessments.

▌ At grade 8, students at each level of parental education had higher scores in 2000 than in 1990. At grade 12, however, only students who reported their parents' highest level of education as "graduated from college" had higher scores in 2000 than in 1990.

TYPE OF SCHOOL

▮ At all three grades in 2000, students attending non-public schools outperformed their peers attending public schools.

▮ Over the period from 1990 to 2000, public, non-public, and Catholic schools had increased average scores for fourth graders. For eighth graders the scores of public, non-public, Catholic, and other non-public school students also increased over the ten-year period. Similarly, for twelfth graders, average scores for all the school types were higher in 2000 than in 1990.

TYPE OF LOCATION

▮ In 2000 fourth, eighth, and twelfth graders in central city schools had lower average scores than their counterparts in urban fringe/large town schools. Fourth and eighth graders in central city schools had lower average scores than their counterparts in rural/small town schools. Fourth graders in urban fringe/large town schools had higher scores than their counterparts in rural/small town schools.

FREE/REDUCED-PRICE LUNCH PROGRAM

▮ At all three grades in 2000, students eligible for the free/reduced-price lunch program administered by the USDA (U.S. Department of Agriculture) had lower average scores than those who were not eligible. Free/reduced-price lunches are intended for children at or near the poverty line: eligibility is determined by the USDA's income eligibility guidelines.

OTHER FINDINGS

▮ In 2000 eighth graders whose teachers majored in either mathematics or mathematics education had higher average scores than did students whose teachers did not major in these subjects.

▮ Most fourth- and eighth-grade students in 2000 were taught by teachers who considered themselves to be well prepared to teach the mathematics content areas assessed by NAEP. There were no significant differences in the average scores of fourth graders based on teachers' self-reported level of preparation in NAEP content areas. However, eighth graders whose teachers reported being very well prepared in these content areas had higher average scores than did students whose teachers reported they were less well prepared.

Reform Efforts Across the Nation

- Eighth graders in 2000 who were taught by mathematics teachers with eleven or more years of experience had higher average scores than those taught by teachers with two years or less of experience.

- Eighth graders whose teachers reported that they permitted unrestricted use of calculators had higher average scores in 2000 than did the students whose teachers restricted calculator use.

- In grades 4, 8, and 12, there was an increase between 1996 and 2000 in the percentage of students in schools that reported computers were available at all times in classrooms.

- Twelfth graders' responses to the NAEP questionnaire in 2000 indicated that 94% had taken first-year algebra, 88% had taken geometry, 18% had taken statistics, and 18% had taken calculus.

- Analysis of course-taking patterns revealed a positive association between higher levels of mathematics courses taken and progressively higher NAEP mathematics scores.

- Fewer eighth and twelfth graders reported liking mathematics in 2000 than in the early 1990s.

**All above data compiled from *The Nation's Report Card: Mathematics 2000*, published by the National Center for Education Statistics, U.S. Department of Education, August 2001.

ANALYSIS

The above data are useful only to the extent that it is clear to the reader that the result of the 2000 mathematics NAEP is similar, if not identical, to the picture painted by results in other subject matter disciplines tested by the NAEP: reading and science. For our purposes we will only be looking at a close analysis of the results of the NAEP testing carried out in two areas: reading and mathematics, for grades 4 and 8. NAEP exams were carried out in mathematics in 1996, 2000, and 2003; in reading in 1994, 1998, and 2003. It is important to note that the NAEP is one of only three nationally (that is, in all fifty states) administered testing instruments. The other two are the SAT (Scholastic Assessment Test) and the ACT (American College Testing Program).

Before we begin the comparison of the two principal subject matters, let us consider some of the implications of the data reported above from the National Center for Education Statistics.

1. While it may be tempting to conclude that there has been some slight increases in mathematics achievement in the United States in the past decade, that conclusion would not be accurate for the following reasons. Even though fourth and eighth graders show sporadic increases in a few instances under certain socioeconomic and regional circumstances, twelfth graders' achievement is either flat, declines, or is not statistically significant. These kinds of results repeat over and over again in the case of other subject matters tested by the NAEP. It is beyond the scope of this book to outline in detail all of the data reported by the NAEP. However, the reader can be assured that under no circumstances have the NAEP results been suggested as a positive guideline for curriculum reform in mathematics, or in any other subject discipline for that matter. Furthermore, the validity and reliability, as previously stated, of the three achievement levels (basic, proficient, and advanced) have not been proved (Manzo and Galley, 2003).
2. Since twelfth graders are at the exit point and represent the culmination of K–12 schooling, it must be interpreted that the results reported by the NAEP indicate nothing less than a lack of success in public schooling as measured by the NAEP over the past ten years in the subject matters of reading, mathematics, and science. Even with the slightly improved outcomes in mathematics in 2003 (outcomes are flat in reading in 2003), the overall reported percentage of students in the proficient range is not encouraging (in math: grade 4: 31%; grade 8: 27% and in reading: grade 4: 30%; grade 8: 30%).
3. It can be extrapolated from the grade 4 and grade 8 data that the percentages of students who scored at or above the proficient range never exceed one-third of the entire population tested. It can be further concluded that the students who agree to take the NAEP exams are a self-selected sampling that does not exactly represent the full array of students in the larger population.
4. The gap between white students' achievement in mathematics and that of black, Hispanic, and American Indian students continues to be problematic and augurs poorly for the future in terms of equity in education.
5. It is disturbing to note that at grade 12 only white students had a higher average score in 2000 than in 1990. Once again, the score gaps between white and all other minority students continue to be not only problematic as noted above but also prevent any kind of systematic improvements to their quality of life if indeed achievement in mathematics is correlated to quality of life. Even the 2003 results

show a stubborn tendency to leave black and Hispanic students well behind their white counterparts (Manzo and Galley, 2003).
6. Parental education has always been viewed as a significant variable in achievement in school. The 2000 results confirm that students whose parents have a higher level of education in fact do better on the NAEP tests. What is of most concern about this finding is that it has already been established in other documents by the NAEP that parental education is most closely correlated to socioeconomic status.
7. It has always been understood that the lunch program of the USDA relates most closely to poverty status and therefore the data reinforce that students who are in this underclass will continue to do poorly in school.

Let us now examine more closely the actual data reported on the NAEP mathematics and reading tests from 1994 to 2003.

Overall Vital Statistics

The overall vital statistics on U.S. public schools are as follows:

Public schools	90,640
Public school teachers	2,988,000
Pre-K–12 students	47,576,000
Annual pre-K–12 expenditures	$358 billion
Minority students	38.6%
Children in poverty	18.9%
Students with disabilities	12.8%
English language learners	8.0%

Achievement in Mathematics: 1996, 2000, and 2003 and Achievement in Reading: 1994, 1998, and 2003

Almost all of the fifty states participate in the NAEP. While a review of all of the data has been completed by this author, the meta-analysis that seems most productive and useful to this particular book is to identify states that have different approaches to standards and accountability and to compare the achievement levels in mathematics and reading of these states. While there is a reasonably large range of achievement levels across the United States, it is peculiar, if not surprising, that there is little or no difference between states that set standards and those who have never done so. For this analysis I will compare the following three states: Iowa, Massachusetts, and Montana, in terms of percentage of students scoring at or above the proficient level.

	IOWA	MASSACHUSETTS	MONTANA
MATHEMATICS ACHIEVEMENT—1996			
4th Grade	22	24	22
8th Grade	31	28	32
MATHEMATICS ACHIEVEMENT—2000			
4th Grade	28	33	25
8th Grade	Unavail.	32	37
MATHEMATICS ACHIEVEMENT—2003			
4th Grade	36	41	31
8th Grade	33	38	35
READING ACHIEVEMENT—1994			
4th Grade	35	36	35
8th Grade	Unavail.	Unavail.	Unavail.
READING ACHIEVEMENT—1998			
4th Grade	35	37	37
8th Grade	Unavail.	36	38
READING ACHIEVEMENT—2003			
4th Grade	35	40	35
8th Grade	36	43	37

Of the above three states, one state, Iowa, has never set standards and accountability and received an F for its standards and accountability category. Massachusetts, in contrast, is at the other end of the spectrum and received an A- for its efforts in the area of standards and accountability. Finally, Montana, which has made some attempts at standards but basically has not made much effort in this regard, also received an F. The grades for these three states are reported for the year 2000. Also, in 1998, Massachusetts received an A for its efforts, Montana received a D, and Iowa received an F.

There is no need to apply any sophisticated statistical analysis to the above numbers that represent the percentage of students who scored at or above the *proficient* level in either mathematics or reading. In fact, in the reading achievement difference, Massachusetts versus Iowa is at most 7% (2003). The mathematics percentages do indicate a slight difference in achievement where Massachusetts is slightly higher than both Iowa and Montana in the fourth grade mathematics achievement, but the percentages actually show fewer students in eighth grade achieving at the *proficient* level than the result in Montana (data from Iowa were unavailable due to lack of participation from this grade). A similar scenario emerges from the eighth grade results in mathematics in 1996 where the Massachusetts result is slightly less than that of both Montana and Iowa; in 2003, the Massachusetts result is slightly higher in math and reading, in both grades, 4 and 8.

The reason for the above analysis, albeit brief, is to emphasize that there is no significant difference between states that spend billions of dollars working on standards and accountability and states that do virtually nothing in this area. I believe that it is important to focus on this fact because, while there is variation across the fifty states in achievement in mathematics and reading, one would expect that there would be a *larger* difference in the extreme cases of states that choose not to engage in setting standards as opposed to states that do spend considerable time, effort, and money on this endeavor. For those who have a sanguine perspective on the future direction of education reform in terms of a focus on setting standards in all fifty states—along with an expenditure of a considerable amount of resources in this effort—there is little evidence to cause any celebration.

The meta-analysis carried out by this author also revealed that the so-called achievement gap between white students and black students or Hispanic students is sizeable enough to cause concern in terms of the question of education reform being an effective vehicle for providing equity in educational opportunity in mathematics and reading in the United States. It is simply not the case that education reform over the past decade has, in any significant way, closed the achievement gap.

Working conditions

Continuing our analysis of the three states compared above in terms of achievement, let us now look at the data on working conditions as reported by the 2003 "Quality Counts" report of *Education Week*. While data were available for all fifty states, the significance of the data is somewhat blurred. The questions that were asked of teachers in the "Quality Counts" 2003 report dealt with the following:

1. Students' disrespect for teachers;
2. Students coming to school unprepared to learn;
3. A lack of parental involvement; and
4. Availability of necessary materials such as textbooks, supplies, and copy machines.

Among the three states compared above, namely Iowa, Massachusetts, and Montana, the differences reported by teachers in these categories are virtually nonexistent, with the ironic exception of question #4, where 69% of teachers in Massachusetts reported that necessary materials were available as compared to Iowa where 83% reported favorably and in Montana 82% reported favorably.

Results of the other three issues noted above are as follows (teachers were asked whether the issue above was either a moderate or a serious problem in their school):

	IOWA	**MASSACHUSETTS**	**MONTANA**
Question 1	45%	41%	43%
Question 2	61%	58%	58%
Question 3	50%	49%	49%

UNFULFILLED EXPECTATIONS

The above analysis of achievement levels, achievement gaps, and working conditions for the fifty states generally and for three states in particular leads us to a conclusion that education reform, as it is now conceived, is indeed systematized across the United States, but this fact of systemization has not yielded the kind of gains that one would have hoped over a full decade of effort. The key point that must be emphasized involves the conceptualization of what education reform should mean and what should be focused on as one goes through an education reform act or legislation in each state. This author has found that there is no evidence to either select one state for its replicability nor is there enough difference between and among states to warrant extensive or intensive analysis of key variables in the fifty states. There simply are no data to justify a search for the model state to be replicated in the other forty-nine. (It is important to state that Massachusetts was selected as a case study [chapter 2] because this author is most familiar with its Education Reform Act of 1993.)

Of course, many other features and variables go into the various reform efforts across the fifty states. It is not the intention of this author to minimize or to revile those efforts. Rather, it is, in the judgment of this author, the responsibility of each state to demonstrate why its education reform efforts have warranted the amount of effort, resources, energy, and money. It is the contention of this author that the amount of gain demonstrated in the data (NAEP data selected, again, due to its widespread use) does not speak to or conjure up a high degree of confidence in the various legislative acts that have dominated the attention of citizens in the United States for more than a decade.

EFFECT OF TECHNOLOGY

In the report "Technology Counts" 2003, published by *Education Week*, there is an attempt to capture the state of technology in the schools in terms of availability of computers and use of technology in instruction. It is the opinion of this author that the report is an interesting analysis of a very important topic but offers little in the way of data by which one might compare states in terms of their technological advances in the schools. Having said this, there is nonetheless a plethora of interesting information about teachers' attitudes toward technology and the effect of technology on instruction so as to warrant a review by any serious student of education reform.

It is the conclusion of this author that technology, in and of itself, has not, and cannot, improve the abysmal conditions present in public education today. This is not to indict any state for its embracing of technology as one of many targets for its education reform efforts. Rather, this analysis of "Technology Counts" 2003 speaks volumes about the enormous difficulty that each state experiences in its attempts to improve public education.

As a way to emphasize the role of technology in the area of education reform, it is interesting to compare the same three states represented above in terms of the percentage of teachers who participate in professional development on the use of computers for instruction (reported for the year 2000). Iowa shows 67% of teachers participating, Massachusetts 68%, and Montana 73%. While there is virtually no statistical difference among these numbers, there is the symbolic significance that there is *once again* no statistically significant difference between a state at the top of the standards-setting hierarchy (Massachusetts) versus the only state that does not and has not ever set standards (Iowa). Montana is represented by a fairly respectable 73%.

The availability of computers and other technical resources as well as the use of technology in instruction are perhaps the two most significant and important areas for future study in the area of the effect of technology on education reform.

DECLINING MEDIOCRITY

Twenty years ago the United States was declared "a nation at risk." At risk educationally, at least ("A Nation at Risk," 1983). President Ronald Reagan charged Secretary of Education Terrel H. Bell with the mandate "to present a report on the quality of education in America." He further charged the secretary of education with making recommendations that would eliminate any deficiencies in education generally and in secondary education in particular. This report has been the lightning rod for many attempts at educational improvement over the past twenty years. There was a sense at the time—indeed there continues to be that sense—that the United States of America was losing ground educationally in comparison to other countries in the world, especially those with which we seek to compare. There was no doubt that the result of the report caused extreme anxiety among educators, policymakers, and others so much so that there has never been one day since the release of this report that we have been "comfortable" with the state of education in this country.

Among the findings of the commission were the following: As many as twenty-three million Americans were illiterate; only one-fifth of 17-year-olds could write a persuasive essay and only a few more could do a simple, two-step math problem; about two-thirds of high school seniors spent less than one hour on homework; a lower proportion of students attended science courses than in other industrial countries; textbooks had become unchallenging and repetitious; and 42% of students had taken "general track" courses that led nowhere (Holton, B13). It has been said that President Reagan used the report as a Trojan horse to help win the 1984 election (Holton, B15). The somber facts were not challenged by many, and gradually but surely a consensus was obtained among most Americans concerning the "rising tide of mediocrity" in American public education.

Considering that we were put on notice twenty years ago that the educational system in the United States was dysfunctional, there should be no surprise that we have fallen further behind internationally in terms of the achievement of our students in core academic subjects. Moreover, we have not effectively dealt with the achievement gap between white students and minority students. A review of the report only highlights the continuous need for education reform in this country. What it does not provide is a guideline for developing a strategy that will, in fact, equalize educational opportunities among all learners. Our focus needs to be on making teaching a true profession and repairing the often disgraceful status of our curriculum, our moral leadership, and the overall outcomes of the educational system in terms of improving the human condition.

CONCLUSION

Gary W. Phillips, Deputy Commissioner at the National Center for Education Statistics in Washington, D.C., reported in the *The Condition of Education* (2002) that:

> Trends in the condition of American education show a mixed picture. While high school graduates have increased their enrollment in more advanced courses since the early 1980s, the performance of twelfth-graders in mathematics and science has stagnated in recent years. International comparisons suggest that U.S. ninth-graders have relatively good civic knowledge and even better civic skills, but that the reading literacy scores of U.S. 15-year-olds are similar to the

international average among advanced industrialized countries. International comparisons in mathematics and science also show mixed results, with U.S. eighth-graders performing above the international average of 38 countries, but below the average of their counterparts in 14 countries.

In addition, gaps persist in academic performance and educational participation among different racial/ethnic groups, socioeconomic groups, and school sectors. The gaps between the average reading scores of white and black students ages 9, 13, and 17 have remained stable or increased since the late 1980s. In mathematics, high poverty levels in schools are associated with low student achievement in the fourth grade. While the percentage of drop-outs in the population of white and black young adults has declined, the percentage for Hispanics has remained higher than that of other groups and remains high.

Finally, private school students in general scored higher than public school students in reading, mathematics, and science. A growing and increasingly diverse population of elementary and secondary students continues to heighten the challenge of providing high-quality instruction and *equal educational opportunities* (emphasis added). In addition, school absence among middle and high school students and the declining academic interest of high school seniors are just a few of the challenges that educators face. (ix)

In recent years federal efforts have largely centered on the NCLB (No Child Left Behind) legislation (2001), which is a public statement on the direction of education reform espoused by the current leadership in Congress as well as by President George W. Bush. For this reason, the law can be viewed as a platform, largely political in nature, for the federal government in terms of its declaration on how to improve public schooling in the United States. In essence, however, we must keep in mind that the NCLB is, for the most part, another reauthorization of the ESEA (Elementary and Secondary Education Act).

Rather than explain the legislation, which can be easily accessed via the Internet (it is PL 107–10 and can be viewed or downloaded at: <www.ed.gov/legislation/ESEA02>), let us examine the major goals of ESEA/NCLB 2001 and discuss their effects and implications.

The goals are:

1. *Accountability for results*
   - Each state can define its own standards but must test every child, grades 3–8, annually in mathematics and reading, by the school year 2005–2006.
   - All schools must show AYP (adequate yearly progress) or else be labeled "in need of improvement."
2. *Emphasis on doing what works based on scientific research*
   - Teacher training a high priority.

- Schools "in need of improvement" must spend at least 10% of Title I funds on improving teacher skills.
- All new teachers must pass competency tests in subject area to be taught.

3. *Expanded parental options*
- Schools "in need of improvement" must offer parents a choice of where child can attend school (defined as two consecutive years not meeting AYP [Title I schools only]).
- Supplemental services must be offered if a school fails to meet AYP standard for three consecutive years.

4. *Expanded local control and flexibility*
- State decides on student testing and teacher testing.
- Districts can use up to 50% of federal monies (from Titles II, IV, V) for teacher quality/improvement initiatives.

There is no question that the NCLB has increased accountability. Yet there is contentious debate among governors concerning how to meet the demands of the new law since the amount of new funds for NCLB initiatives has been extremely small or nonexistent. In fact, the legislation stalled in the U.S. Senate due to disagreement over the whole issue of AYP, eventually ending up with a new AYP formula prior to its passing.

On the matter of scientific research guiding curriculum and instruction, it would be foolhardy to believe that any agreement exists on how to best implement school programs. In fact, as we will see in part II of this book, the issue of what is available for use versus what is actually used in classrooms provides a disturbing portrayal of how the local agencies (districts and states) fail to access the resources available to them. Add to this scene an overlay of federal mandate and it requires little imagination to predict what many practitioners are already saying about the effectiveness of NCLB: it seems more to be the epitome of leaving all children behind in terms of any serious attempt to reform public schooling in the United States.

Expanded parental options can never really be realized without a concomitant proviso for transportation to any school chosen. Also, as we will see in chapter 2, experiments in school reform in New Zealand may offer a sober warning when it comes to relying on "market forces" to close poor-performing schools while trying to help the surviving schools flourish. And as for local control, how effective is it to require enormous amounts of testing (for students and teachers), fund almost none of it, and hold schools accountable for demonstrating adequate yearly progress? This new NCLB bill puts many critical issues far behind in priority and leaves no child in any better shape than he or she was before NCLB.

Indeed, the challenges that will present themselves in the future are enormous. In the next chapter we take a close look at reform in one state—Massachusetts.

CHAPTER 2

A CLOSE LOOK AT REFORM IN ONE STATE
The Massachusetts Experiment

> The Commonwealth now has a new Commissioner of Education . . . and a new Chairman of the Board of Education. Now we need to return to the work of implementing education reform.
> —Perry P. Davis, President of the Massachusetts Association of School Superintendents, Newsletter, March 1999

REFORM (VERB) IS, ACCORDING TO *Webster's Thesaurus* (1994, 194), synonymous with *ameliorate, amend, better, change, correct, help, improve, mend, rectify, renew, right.* To say that American education was, and continues to be, in need of all of the above actions seems, to most reasonable people, a truism. Let us take a closer look at the situation in terms of one state, Massachusetts.

The above quotation is a prominent (first page) opening statement from a leader in an affluent Massachusetts school district. The newsletter appeared in March 1999, six years after the Act to Establish the Education Reform Act of 1993 was legislated in Massachusetts. The act was originally for a period of seven years, that is, ending in the year 2000. The previous commissioner had resigned his post to accept the presidency of a distance-learning company in

Pennsylvania. Thus, as if reform were some easily quantifiable concept, the state then "returned" in 1999 to its reform efforts. It is helpful to delineate the changes embodied in the act.

THE FOLLOWING OUTLINE SPEAKS TO THE MAIN AREAS THAT WERE ADDRESSED WITHIN THE LAW

Under the governance of Massachusetts schools in the years prior to the 1993 Education Reform Act, school committees had general charge of all the public schools within its jurisdiction. Under the new act of 1993, the school committee had essentially the following powers vested in it:

—To select and terminate superintendent
—To review and approve the budget
—To establish educational goals and policies consistent with the requirements of law and statewide goals and standards established by the Board of Education

The above three delineate the *major* powers vested in the school committee.

SPECIFIC POWERS VESTED IN THE SCHOOL COMMITTEES INCLUDE THE FOLLOWING

1. School committees can provide supplemental standards in employee evaluation (chapter 71, section 38).
2. School committees may prescribe additional qualifications for the employment of teachers (section 38G).
3. School committees may adopt and implement a professional development plan for professional employees (section 38Q).
4. School committees retain the power: to change school books by a two-thirds vote; to appoint physicians and nurses; to establish and appoint position of assistant or associate superintendent upon recommendation of the superintendent; have general charge of schoolhouses (sections 47, 50, 53, and 68, respectively).
5. School committees continue to have the duty and authority to bargain collectively with school employees (except for principals) but the city or town CEO is involved in the process.

SPECIFIC POWERS VESTED IN THE SUPERINTENDENT OF SCHOOLS INCLUDE THE FOLLOWING

1. Superintendent publishes policies for the conduct of students and teachers and reviews student expulsions.
2. Superintendent causes evaluations to be conducted district wide.
3. Superintendent awards early professional teacher status and has the exclusive authority to terminate a principal.

4. Superintendent may review principal's decision on termination or demotion of an employee; superintendents also have the power to dismiss any employee in the school district; and superintendent may lay off teachers.
5. Superintendent reviews suspensions initiated by principals or may also initiate suspensions.
6. Superintendent hires coaches in all cases without consultation of any other administrator.
7. Superintendent manages the system consistent with law and consistent with policy decisions of the school committee.
8. Superintendent appoints principals and other administrative staff.

GENERAL NARRATIVE

Sections 37H, 38, 41, 42, 42D, 47A, 59, and 59B contain the full narrative and the law that governs the above powers that are vested in the superintendents under the law.

POWERS VESTED IN PRINCIPALS INCLUDE THE FOLLOWING

1. In section 42 of the law principals are given the power to dismiss or demote any teacher or any other person assigned full-time to the school (in cases where an employee travels to more than one school, the superintendent has the power to dismiss or demote).
2. In section 42D principals are given the power to suspend teachers and other employees who are assigned to the school.
3. In section 48 principals are allowed to purchase school texts subject to the direction of the superintendent (please note that this provision is also subject to the corollary power of the school committee that allows it to change textbooks by a two-thirds vote as previously noted).
4. In section 59B principals have the power: to manage the school, to hire and terminate all building staff subject to superintendent's approval; to promote participatory decision making with professional staff.
5. In section 59C principals have the duty to co-chair and coordinate school councils and create a school improvement plan.
6. In section 59D, along with the superintendent, principals are given the duty to pursue school community partnerships.

POWERS VESTED IN THE SCHOOL COUNCILS INCLUDE THE FOLLOWING

The new education law required that all schools create a school council that is composed of parents selected by the PTO or other reasonable process, teachers, and community persons who are not teachers or parents. Also, in grades 9 to 12, a student sits on the school councils. They are organized by the principal subject to the direction of the superintendent of schools and the duties of the council are to convene under the open meeting law within forty days of the start of a school year and assist in the identification of educational needs of students. The council is also to assist in the review of the annual budget and assist in formulating a school improvement plan subject to school committee review.

The specific powers described above are and were an essential feature of the education reform effort in Massachusetts. Clearly the realignment or redistribution of power under any circumstance is usually viewed as a positive step in the reorganization and improvement of schooling. It should be noted that, for the most part, the superintendent of schools is the key player in all of the now codified reform efforts for the following reason: The superintendent of schools is the person who hires principals who evaluate teachers. While school committees hire superintendents and usually provide multiyear contracts, they are political bodies that change based on the will of the people in the community. For this reason the superintendent is viewed as the more stable figure. It is clear over the several years of education reform in Massachusetts that superintendents have been vested with the most power in terms of the law itself. Interestingly, along with this increased power has come a corollary phenomenon of a shortage of qualified superintendents to fill openings.

Billions of dollars have been spent on education in Massachusetts since the beginning of the Education Reform Act. Over the past seven years, most of the money has gone toward *maintenance* of the facilities, curriculum, and personnel that existed prior to the act in 1993. The increased monies that have been sent to school districts have had the greatest impact on professional development programs that have been instituted to support the improvement of teacher performance in the classroom. Little impact can be identified, however, in terms of learning outcomes.

It has been tacitly understood that behind any improvement efforts within Massachusetts schools lies the unspoken truth that standards exist to guide these efforts. Carl Glickman of the University of Georgia lists the positive aspects of these standards (Glickman, 2000, 7). He states that there is an emphasis on standards that every child is expected to achieve at higher levels than ever before, and teachers and schools will be publicly responsible for proving that this can be done. In fact, Massachusetts has created curriculum frameworks that have always had the intended target of increasing the expectations of teachers in classrooms and concomitantly increasing the achievement levels of students because of that greater focus on standards. However, as we saw in chapter 1, it is questionable whether an increase in standards *causes* an increase in achievement.

As far as proving whether this kind of activity in fact improves student learning, a set of tests called the MCAS (Massachusetts Comprehensive Assessment System) has provided core subject matter assessments in grades 4, 8, and 10 (with additional grades added as of 2001). The results of the MCAS testing have yielded a rank ordering of all schools in the state. Approximately ninety of these schools, according to the Massachusetts Department of Education, have been targeted for additional help because their results on these tests have been abysmally low. The state has created teams who will go in and consult on a technical basis with school districts to address the leadership, curriculum delivery, and assessment of students in that school. After two years of help at a particular school, the state has the right to "take over" that school. At the present time, there are two school districts that have been labeled "underachieving" and two others targeted for increased monitoring (that is, so-called "watch" status).

Now while there have been no formal takeovers with the possible exception of Lawrence, Massachusetts, which underwent intense scrutiny by the state from 2000 to 2002, there has been a number of schools that have been targeted for technical assistance. It is less important to cite the actual numbers of schools that might be subject to state scrutiny than it is to ask the question: Have the standards established by the state, that is, the curriculum frameworks and the MCAS testing as well as the changes in the governance of the schools meant that children have achieved at higher levels than they did prior to the Education Reform Act?

While there is no easy answer to this question, what is clear is that the controversy surrounding the curriculum and the testing has created a lot of tension within Massachusetts school districts and has directed a lot of attention toward education and schooling. Of course this phenomenon can be seen throughout the United States, and it is not uncommon that a standard (such as Glickman's emphasis that every child is expected to achieve at higher levels) is explicitly incorporated in various states' laws. Glickman also states that in some accountability systems there is a greater targeting of resources and funds to the schools where students are not achieving at the specified level (7). In other words, funding ends up tied to achievement as measured by standardized tests.

What seems to prevent or obviate the accomplishments, or the meeting of standards, is a number of variables, admittedly irksome yet omnipresent, that make themselves felt in any human enterprise that tries to alter teaching and learning. For example, as Glickman notes, standards contribute to the exercise of unilateral state control in all operational aspects of schools (7). In fact, the attempt to improve schools almost always concentrates the ultimate evaluative decisions at the state level. The notion of state level control seems to fly in the face of all good empirical evidence that the locus of control ought to be in fact at the school, or at the very least, the district level. In addition, in some states the narrowness of the standards that are established for every academic discipline and the subsequent single format tests give rise to a level of mastery that is indeed suspect by any stretch of the evaluative imagination. Not only is it difficult to measure discrete level knowledge and measure it well, it has been increasingly impossible to report the results as being reliable and valid once testing is carried out. In fact, in Massachusetts the MCAS testing has been challenged by a group of professors at Boston College, which has questioned the reliability and validity of MCAS and has challenged the notion of using high-stakes testing to determine whether one graduates from high school, which in Massachusetts began with the class of 2003.

It seems reasonable enough to question the use of one single measure to decide whether one receives a high school diploma. It also raises another important question, namely whether the content was a fair selection from an important domain of knowledge. Indeed, all too often the content itself and the level of mastery sought are based on one group's idea of what every student needs to learn by a certain time. For example, in Massachusetts the high school graduating class of 2003 faced the daunting task of passing both the mathematics and the English MCAS tests in order to receive their diplomas. Of the approximately 950,000 students in Massachusetts, about 70,000 are tenth graders in high school. The students had to pass the English and mathematics portion of the MCAS tests in order to receive a diploma in the year 2003. While given the opportunity to retake these tests up to five times between sophomore and senior year, it is not too far fetched to presume that many students in fact drop out of high school once of legal age rather than face multiple failures on the same measure. It is precisely this issue—*namely failure on a single test*—that presents itself as the largest obstacle to a successful reform effort.

The passing score for the MCAS has been determined to be a score of 220 on a scale ranging from 200 to 280. Failure is defined as a score between 200 and 219, and 220 is the lowest point on the second range, namely 220 to 239, which is characterized as "needs improvement." To be "proficient," one needs to score between 240 and 259, and to be deemed "advanced," one would have to attain a score between 260 and 280. The State of Massachusetts Board of Education voted in the spring of 2000 to set 220 as the passing score in order to receive a high school diploma. Some board members challenged whether it was a good idea to face the inevitable failure rates (and perhaps dropout rates as well) that most certainly were an inevitable part of those high-stakes measures.

Furthermore, based on past performance, approximately one out of four students will fail one or both tests on the first try (Massachusetts Department of Education). Now it should be noted and emphasized that these failure rates are determined by an arbitrary score that is considerably low, namely the score of 220 on a scale that ranges from 200 to 280. The Board of Education in Massachusetts set the passing score at 220 in order to give a reasonable number of students a fair chance to pass the test.

Let us now return to the issue of standards. Glickman names three other areas that highlight negative aspects of standards. The three are: (1) single criterion testing is poor science; (2) many states provide no allowance for what is called prototype schools or districts that can develop their own standards and assessments to challenge the state's system of accountability, which in essence declares *the one* model of what it means to be well educated; and (3) there is a question of whether accountability systems offer a reasonable definition of what it means to be well educated and whether that should be mandated such that all schools conform to the state's definition(Glickman, 2000). Of course, these three arguments are restatements of concerns that many reasonable people might have. However, there is more to the problem.

Thomas Newkirk, a professor of English at the University of New Hampshire, writes in an article entitled "A Mania for Rubrics: Will the Standards Movement Make Satire (and Good Writing) Obsolete?" In the article Newkirk talks about the film *Dead Poets Society,* where Robin Williams plays an English teacher who, midway through having students read from an absurd preface to their anthology of poetry (which stated that a work of literature can be evaluated by graphing two qualities, namely importance and execution), tells the students to rip out the offending pages. Newkirk goes on to point out that this movie's warning is still relevant today because "We are now in the middle of a resurgence of mechanical instruction in writing" (2000, 41). The article does a very good job of pointing out how rubrics restrict creativity.

While it is debatable whether there is a need for a specific set of criteria in order to judge students' work, Newkirk, nonetheless, demonstrates quite well that the more sophisticated and higher order kinds of writing, usually valued, end up undetectable when one defines too clearly what the rubrics should seek. Put another way, rubrics sometimes establish predetermined weighting systems that define whether a piece of writing has met certain so-called criteria that have been deemed important. (For example, organization, detail, and mechanics are three criteria that rubrics frequently address.) Newkirk tells the reader how the obsession with rubrics has silenced the creative voice. As he points out, "Rubrics fail to provide a *demonstration* of the reading process that can be later internalized by the writer" (41). The author ends by very adeptly characterizing the evaluation problems that arise in using rubrics. He points out how the authoritative language and format of rubrics tend to hide the human act of writing. He goes on to say that "The key qualities of good writing ... are represented as something the writing *has*—rather than something the writing *does*" (41).

A good example is provided by Newkirk to show how one teacher, a kindergarten teacher, prepared her students for a drawing test. The article that he quotes is drawn from the February 2000 issue of *Educational Leadership,* and he quotes exactly as follows:

> After the teacher explained what elements of the drawing were needed to get a score of four, she said, "Notice that this drawing shows the ground colored green and brown. There are also a tree, the sky, some clouds and the sun." She then showed a picture earning a three in which the tree, clouds, and sun were not as clearly defined. After this explanation, she asked each student to create artwork that met the requirement of the level four drawing and rate the artwork of a partner. Children spent the rest of the class concluding their drawings until all the student pictures either met the level four rubric or went up at least one level. (41)

This kind of preparation for a test or any kind of instructional task is developmentally inappropriate. And while we may not want to go as far as to characterize it as "educational malpractice" (41), it clearly sacrifices creativity for the sake of meeting standards-based instruction, which is why, according to Newkirk, the standards movement is going to make satire obsolete.

DEGREE OF SUCCESS IN MASSACHUSETTS EDUCATION REFORM

Massachusetts has made a sincere attempt to improve the schools by establishing standards, creating curriculum frameworks, and testing the content that the new education reform act set out to define. While there is absolutely nothing wrong with these kinds of efforts, an important question to ask is how these efforts may measure up to a more generic view of how successful reform might take place. An interesting set of propositions about successful reform can be found in the February 9, 2000, issue of *Education Week,* in an article entitled "Foundations for Change" written by Richard H. Hersh (2000), who was formerly the president of Hobart and William Smith Colleges in Geneva, New York, and is now the director of grant programs at the Christian A. Johnson Endeavor Foundation in New York City. His books include *Promoting Moral Growth: From Piaget to Kohlberg* (1979); *Models of Values and Moral Education* (1980); and *The Structure of School Reform* (1983). In this article Hersh talks about America's concern for its public schools and how since the 1957 launch of Sputnik, attempts at education reform have been plentiful and numerous. For example, with the 1983 report from the federal government "A Nation at Risk," we have seen two decades of vigorous activity toward improving the educational enterprise in the United States. As Hersh points out, "As we enter this new century, we are a nation at greater risk because we understand that schooling excellence is a necessary condition for Democratic citizenship, social justice, and individual, as well as collective, economic security in a global and technologically sophisticated world" (2000, 60).

Hersh says further that "Individuals who cannot read or write well, who have no sense of the major human questions, who cannot think critically or act morally and who show little interest in continuing to learn will be the severely disadvantaged of the future, as well as the larger community" (60). He goes on to point out that in spite of the difficulty in changing the educational enterprise, there are generalizations around reform efforts that can lead us to a set of common attributes of successful reform. The following is a list of these attributes (40):

1. *Clear goals and high expectations and standards*
The higher the expectations and standards, the higher the achievement. Teachers, administrators, and school board reach a consensus on these issues.

2. *Tightly coupled curriculum*
Learning objects, curriculum materials, teaching strategies, evaluation, and rewards are purposely linked as a whole, each component connected to and reinforcing the others.

3. *Community support*
Parents must affirm a culture of excellence in each school and classroom—by supporting it at home and expecting the same high standards as the school board, teachers, and administrators, as well as actively participate in the life of the schools.

4. *Respectful and orderly environment*
Learning in school requires a safe, orderly, and equitable environment. Disruption and disrespect for other individuals or property are not tolerated.

5. *Academic learning time*
The more time students are actively engaged in appropriate learning tasks, the greater and deeper the learning.

6. *Frequent and monitored homework*
Homework connected to school lessons reinforced by teacher attention to that homework increases academic learning time and promotes independent and cooperative learning.

7. *Teacher competence*
Teachers who possess an extensive and rich repertoire of skills and knowledge do in fact promote greater learning than these of marginal competence.

8. *Pervasive caring*
High-achieving schools are rigorous and caring places. Teachers and staff members genuinely care about each student and care enough to demand a student's best efforts.

9. *Frequent assessment of student achievement*
Student learning is constantly assessed both formally and informally to provide timely feedback to students and to help teachers and the school revise curriculum and pedagogy.

10. *Public rewards and incentives*
Student achievement is publicly held as the highest value and is publicly celebrated through the use of oral and written comments, honors assemblies, displays of student work, media attention, and communication to parents.

11. *Administrative leadership*
The most effective schools have administrators in the school and at the district level possessing the skills and courage that demand and help create the ten conditions just listed.

Massachusetts in its Education Reform Act demonstrates some of the above attributes. In other cases, it falls short.

Let us consider the Massachusetts experiment vis-à-vis the above attributes of successful reform.

First of all, the first attribute: clear goals and high expectations and standards. The issue of whether there is consensus on the expectations and standards used in the Education Reform Act of 1993 is doubtful. As a matter of fact, consensus has been hard to come by as evidenced by the amount of disruption, instability, and indecision around key issues such as curriculum frameworks, tests, and other highly visible and important issues of reform. Although it is perhaps too early to judge whether Massachusetts has demonstrated clear goals, it is not too early to point out that if consensus is a feature of meeting clear goals, then Massachusetts clearly has a long way to go to find and demonstrate this attribute.

The second attribute: tightly coupled curriculum. The curriculum frameworks of Massachusetts were not fully operational until 1998, a full five years into the reform act. Since that time, there has been confusion, particularly in the social studies/history and science/technology curriculum frameworks. Once the board voted the English and mathematics frameworks, there was immediate reaction to mathematics whereby a major organization, the National Council of Teachers of Mathematics, questioned whether the framework was regressive rather than progressive.

As if that were not bad enough, the other curriculum frameworks were either incomplete or too controversial to take to a vote. The social studies/history framework is a particularly good example of the politics of curriculum at the state level since there was a faction that wanted more world history and less Eurocentric history. And there was another faction that wanted a clear-cut focus on Western civilization. There was a long stalemate on this curriculum, leaving the teachers and the schools to fend for themselves.

While the Board of Education did the right thing in not requiring passing this framework in order to graduate, it nonetheless showed less than admirable administrative leadership in waiting so long to decide on such an important matter.

As for the other frameworks, at the end of the year 2000, the board revised again the science and technology curriculum framework to include a K through 12 strand of engineering tasks. It has voted on several others and plans to have tests in all subject areas.

Clearly, the continual revision and hesitation to publish curriculum guides at the state level can only cause confusion and resentment in the schools, and in Massachusetts, while it is not clear the extent to which the curriculum frameworks are implemented or not, it is clear by the results of the MCAS testing that much of the content of these frameworks is either not being taught or is inadequately learned by the students. The question that will be a key one is whether there are any instructional strategies that have been implemented in Massachusetts schools in order to teach students to master the content and skills embedded in the curriculum frameworks. (This matter will be taken up fully in chapter 6.)

As far as community support, it is difficult to assess to what extent parents have supported the Board of Education. It is presumed that high-performing school districts, that is, upper-middle-class suburbs of Boston, for example, continue to witness a high degree of parental activity and support, whereas in the urban centers, the level of parental support has not changed, that is, it has remained very low. While it has almost come to a point of being "acceptable" that these conditions exist, it is nonetheless an adjudication, albeit quite early, that the Massachusetts reform effort has not substantially changed the level of community support.

This author has spent more than 35,000 hours in schools, as a teacher, an administrator, and an evaluator, and during this time, which has included the seven-year period of education reform in Massachusetts, it has been anecdotally documented that the learning environment within many schools is one that is not safe, orderly, or equitable. Disruption and disrespect seem rampant, and the level of regard of one individual for another seems to be woefully lacking. While I would not indict the Board of Education of Massachusetts for creating this kind of environment, I would note strongly that the education reform act has not addressed this attribute at all.

In terms of learning time, the Education Reform Act of Massachusetts actively took on this issue in a document entitled "Time and Learning" (Massachusetts Department of Education, 1993). The Board of Education did address time on tasks and instructional time issues and concluded that all schools should endeavor to increase the amount of instructional time that students were actively engaged in learning.

On the issue of homework, most school districts have taken a proactive stance on this issue and codified the amount of homework that each grade should have. The question of whether the school enforces homework, or whether parents support the activity of doing homework, is yet to be researched at the empirical level.

Teacher competence has been addressed in Massachusetts in terms of recertification, or, as it is now called, licensure. In order to renew a teacher's license in Massachusetts, one must accumulate a minimum of 120 PDPs (professional development points) during a five-year cycle. The points can be accumulated through any relevant course work, seminars, workshops, and so forth. And for each additional area in which one wants to be certified, the candidate must demonstrate additional PDPs. Indeed, the first cycle of recertification in Massachusetts occurred in 1999. At that time all teachers were required to submit evidence of professional development or leave their certification inactive. In terms of teacher competence, it is patently clear that the accumulation of professional points in most cases will not enhance a basic competence level unless the professional activity is directly related to the competency area. Thus a mathematics teacher who accumulates points in workshops that are not in fact on the improvement of mathematics knowledge will not demonstrate increased competency in his or her teaching area.

This author does not wish to imply that it is not of value for teachers to pursue areas of interest, but essential competence is only enhanced through substantial and highly engaged learning activities. It is not typical that one's competence would be radically changed through a series of brief seminars. Therefore, the Massachusetts Education Reform Act has begun to address the bureaucratic issue of how to license teachers, but it has not addressed the more complicated issue of increasing the overall competency of the entire teaching force of Massachusetts.

I should also note that the Board of Education approved a series of alternative routes to licensure, and these alternative routes are intended to attract nonprofessional teachers, or professionals who wish to make a career change from business or industry to teaching.

Pervasive caring as a concept is of course one that we all seek and many schools believe they have achieved. It is clear, however, that it takes more than caring simply whether students come to school and do their work. As Hersh points out, the most productive aspects of this concept have more to do with demanding student's best effort as opposed to simply caring about a student's welfare. The Massachusetts Education Reform Act does not address this attribute. It is almost as if the idea of caring is not one deemed important enough to be a part of the legislation. What I mean is the legislation seems to take for granted the fact that teachers care about students, that teachers who are professional will genuinely care whether students come to school, do their work, and so forth. But the attribute nature of caring involves more than simply "being nice." It is a more engaging, deeper, and profound sentiment and mentality that a teacher might carry around in dealing with students, seeing students as individuals who are worth a lot of effort and who will achieve at high levels *because of the school and the teacher.*

Frequent assessment of student achievement is a truism within the education profession. It is only questionable whether the staff of a school cares enough about assessment to carry it out constantly in order to give students timely feedback and to use the feedback and data to revise the curriculum and pedagogy of the school.

Concerning public rewards and incentives, the idea that student achievement is publicly held at the highest value is publicly celebrated through the use of oral and written comments, honors assemblies, displays of student work, media attention, and communication to parents. It is clear that the public acknowledgment of achievement is a positive attribute and one that should be sought. What is questionable here is whether the efforts in Massachusetts under the reform act have given rise to a system of too few rewards and too many punitive incentives.

What is patently clear is that the publication of the MCAS results and the ranking of schools create a reward system for wealthy communities who, with or without the reform effort, continue to perform at very high levels. In other words, the MCAS is an incentive for high-performing school districts to continue doing what the systems did all along. However, for urban schools the same publication of test data ends up being a disincentive because urban schools that habitually perform at the lower end continue to do so, and they do not have any incentive to improve. What happens, in essence, is that the embarrassment factor is more powerful than the intention to motivate competition among schools.

Administrative leadership is the last attribute. The most effective schools have administrators who possess the kind of courage to demand and help create the conditions that foster all of the above ten attributes.

It is useful to note that the reform efforts in Massachusetts are not unique and what Massachusetts has endeavored to do in terms of administrative hierarchy and in terms of reform of the schools is shared widely throughout the other forty-nine states. This author has investigated the reform efforts across the country and has found similar patterns across all states (as we saw in chapter 1). Moreover, it is useful to cite efforts in other countries since reform of schooling is not unique to the United States. In New Zealand, for example, there is a reform effort that is called Tomorrow's Schools Reform Movement, and it is useful to look at what has been done there since 1989. An article in *Education Week,* May 17, 2000, entitled "A Distant Laboratory: Learning Cautionary Tales from New Zealand Schools" by Edward B. Fiske and Helen F. Ladd provides insights. Mr. Fiske is the former education editor of the *New York Times,* and Helen F. Ladd is a professor of public policy studies and economics at Duke University. Their book (2001) *When Schools Compete: A Cautionary Tale* was published by the Brookings Institution Press. The following lessons come out of the 2000 article (38):

1. *Self-governance, parental choice, and competition have genuine benefits.*

The majority of primary and secondary schools in New Zealand made a successful transition to self-governance. In New Zealand the decentralization of educational services appealed greatly to parents and parental choice was a popular addition to the educational landscape. In Massachusetts, in contrast, there is a limited choice program that allows school committees to vote to accept students from other communities into their schools assuming there is space to accommodate these additional students. There are financial incentives for communities to do this since the per-pupil expenditure follows the student into the receiving school district thus increasing the overall amount of money available to the district. Since transportation is not a feature of the program, most families shy away from taking advantage of it.

2. *Choice and competition are likely to polarize enrollment patterns by race, ethnicity, socioeconomic status, and student performance.*

The lesson to be learned from New Zealand's Tomorrow's Schools Reform Movement is that choice was more likely to be exercised by upper-class privileged families who learned how to work the system to their advantage. While students from poorer families were represented in the choice program, it turned out that students from disadvantaged backgrounds ended up overrepresented among the noncompetitive schools, thus creating a polarized system of choice.

In the case of Massachusetts it is interesting to note that efforts dating back to the 1970s to desegregate schools have led to several experiments in choice programs as well as magnet schools and other initiatives. In all cases in Massachusetts, programs that have tried to build in choice have not succeeded in desegregating schools nor have they equalized the distribution of resources across school districts. New Zealand's choice program, while at a stage of further development than the Massachusetts' program, is nonetheless a guidepost to avoid spending effort and time in developing choice programs that do not succeed.

3. *Do not count on market forces in and of themselves to solve the problems of troubled urban schools.*

Those in education in Massachusetts know quite well that market forces have not improved the educational programs for two reasons: (1) there is a limited amount of choice built into the system in Massachusetts; and (2) where choice exists, very few citizens actually take advantage of it. As Fiske and Ladd point out, "The concept of an educational marketplace presumes that some competitors will succeed and others will fail." We know all too well based on the eventual fate of many businesses that it is inevitable that a free market economic system will produce schools that will eventually go out of business. The problem then is what to do with the schools that are closed because of poor performance. Clearly it creates a new set of problems for the system as a whole, and these problems are rarely dealt with in Massachusetts or, indeed, nationwide. What this author has discovered in researching the status of education reform efforts across the fifty states is that in no instance could it be found that there was a stopgap measure to assist failing schools.

While it is tempting to believe that closing schools down in and of itself will improve the schools that remain open, there is nonetheless a fiscal and operational reality that says these open schools will be overcrowded, and, therefore, the resources of the remaining schools will be strained.

In New Zealand "The spiraling urban schools had everything that marketers say you need to be successful. They had operational freedom. They had strong incentives to improve teaching and learning in order to avoid losing students. And, at least in quite a few cases, they had strong management."

Yet it is a reality that many schools in New Zealand faced odds that they were unable to overcome and, in fact, ended up becoming losers in the educational marketplace. The lesson that is to be learned then is that we must anticipate the phenomenon of the marketplace and realize that, while it will indeed apply to school choice programs, the resultant effect, namely the closing of many schools, is a much greater problem than the closing, for example, of a retail outlet where customers simply shift over to another store that has survived.

4. *U.S. charter schools can best serve the cause of promoting innovation if they remain limited in number.*

More than with choice programs, the charter school movement has experienced a considerable boom over the past decade. In fact in Massachusetts there was only one charter school in 1992, and, as we began the new century, there were more than fifty. In New Zealand the operational freedom that was introduced into the system tended to produce a variety of types of schools. For example, one school in New Zealand was organized around Howard Gardner's theory of multiple intelligences.

As we learn from New Zealand's Tomorrow's School experiment, as the number of charter schools increases, the tendency to bureaucratize the system is strong. In other words, if charter schools equal the number of "regular" public schools, then what will surface is *a bureaucratic system to manage and operate these schools.* New Zealand's experience demonstrates clearly that "there are limits on the extent to which a government, even one run by political conservatives who are philosophically opposed to big government, will tolerate diversity. As long as charter schools are limited in number, states and local school districts in America can readily assure that the schools are spending tax dollars in a responsible way through the chartering and renewal process. As the number expands, however, greater government regulation is the likely outcome. A large charter school bureaucracy is likely to behave like any other bureaucracy."

5. *Private school vouchers will create the same problems as other market solutions.*

New Zealand has what has been described as a "quasi voucher" system whereby parents exercised choice and a school's revenue was tied to the number of students attracted to that particular school. There is no reason to think that moving to a full voucher system here in the United States would not have the same effects as we observed in New Zealand. While Massachusetts has not endeavored to embark on a full-fledged voucher system (Cleveland, Ohio, and Milwaukee, Wisconsin, have had some experimentation with varying results), it is nonetheless tempting to believe that the next logical step in Massachusetts beyond the Education Reform Act of 1993 is to experiment with full-fledged voucher systems. However, as it was learned in New Zealand, voucher systems carry the same market hazards as all other innovative programs for providing choice due mainly to increasing bureaucracy, centralized control, and lack of real choice for precisely the population that these programs are intended to serve most—low income and poor families.

6. *Mechanisms are needed to balance the interests of various stakeholders.*

New Zealand's approach to centralization failed to provide adequate mechanisms for balancing the interests of the various stakeholders in the state education system by narrowly defining the community that local schools serve. The system pitted schools against one another and against broader interest. The lesson learned in New Zealand, in essence, is that there are many stakeholders involved in the educational enterprise and each stakeholder has his or her own interest in providing more opportunity in choosing a school. Human nature being what it is, it is not surprising that schools experience the same sorts of special interests lobbying that other enterprises do. Therefore, Massachusetts needs to be particularly alerted to the fact that, given its long history of aggressive political action at the state level, we should be very wary and very cautious as we proceed to provide expanded opportunities for how we deliver educational services to the citizens of the state.

CONCLUSION

What we tend to learn from a view of reform efforts across the United States and abroad is that there will always be conflicting forces more than ready to either enhance or deter the efforts to reform and improve educational services. In Massachusetts the Education Reform Act, as noted above, tended to focus on personnel, financial resources, curriculum, and testing. It was especially noted that the vast majority of effort was toward the reorganization of the hierarchy of leadership within the school systems themselves. It was also noted that school committees tended to take on less power, while superintendents took on more. Teachers, it seems, have been the least consulted constituency in all of this effort, even though the state has produced curriculum frameworks with committees established to review and guide the development of these guides. Very few teachers have been involved in the production of the new curriculum that is required in all schools in Massachusetts.

Furthermore, the MCAS tests, as noted above, have tended to create controversy in terms of the validity and reliability of the tests as well as the use of the results. This kind of high-stakes testing, it was noted, creates a sort of ranking of school systems, and, therefore, it simply reinforces the systems that are doing well and further embarrasses those that are not. It is difficult to be excited about continued reform efforts in Massachusetts that ignore the lessons learned from other states and/or other countries.

While the solution to the problem of improving schools is not an easy one, it should be clear by now that the important questions have not been answered, or perhaps even asked. Questions such as *To what extent do we improve the actual delivery of curriculum in classrooms day-to-day so that all students succeed?* is one that has not been answered. Likewise, the question *To what extent are we able to measure whether students have learned what we intended them to learn?* has not been satisfactorily answered.

The experiment in Massachusetts has been revealing and should provide rich foundation for the future efforts to improve its schools and to provide the citizens and students with the kind of educational program of which everyone can be proud. There is a lot of work to do in Massachusetts, as is the case across the nation.

This author has found, as was noted in chapter 1, that reform efforts across the country show less than laudable results. In the pages that follow there will be close examination of the issue of curriculum, instruction, and assessment and of how these areas of concern need the most focus.

CHAPTER 3

RESULTS REDUCED TO NUMBERS
The Race to Show Achievement Gains

IN THIS CHAPTER I WILL ATTEMPT to show that most claims concerning education reform are, in fact, reduced to the reporting of standardized test results. This multibillion-dollar industry has swelled to a point where it has taken over the psyche of the American public in terms of how the average citizen views the success or failure of schools. And, as we have seen in chapter 1, there is no shortage of data, and the average citizen is besieged daily with even more news about how schools are failing.

Alfie Kohn in a commentary in *Education Week*, September 27, 2000, attacks standardized testing as well as its victims (students) and gives some compelling arguments based in fact. His arguments are summed up in the following list of facts.

1. *Our children are tested to an extent that is unprecedented in our history and unparalleled anywhere else in the world.*

2. *Noninstructional factors explain most of the variance among test scores when schools or districts are compared.*

For example, a study of math results on the 1992 NAEP—National Assessment of Educational Progress—found that the combination of four such variables (number of parents living at home, parents' educational background, type of community, and poverty rate) accounted for a whopping 89% of the differences in state scores. Kohn claims that all such analyses of state tests have found comparable results, with the number varying only slightly as a function of which socioeconomic variables were considered (60).

3. *Norm-referenced tests were never intended to measure the quality of learning or teaching.*

Kohn claims that the SAT, MAT, and CAT (Stanford, Metropolitan, and California Achievement Tests) as well as the ITBS and CTBS (Iowa and Comprehensive Tests of Basic Skills), are designed so that only about half the test takers will respond correctly to most items. The main objective of these tests is to rank, not to rate; to spread out the scores, not to gauge the quality of a given student or school.

4. *Standardized test scores often measure superficial thinking.*

Kohn cites evidence from research in educational psychology journals that shows that students who demonstrated superficial thinking skills performed better than their counterparts who were actively engaged in questioning themselves while they read and who tried to connect what they were doing to past learning. As a rule, standardized test results are positively correlated with a shallow approach to learning (46).

5. *Virtually all specialists condemn the practice of giving standardized tests to children younger than eight or nine years old.*

6. *Virtually all relevant experts and organizations condemn the practice of basing important decisions, such as graduation or promotion, on the results of a single test.*

7. *The time, energy, and money that are being devoted to preparing students for standardized tests have to come from somewhere.*

Kohn claims that anyone who doubts the scope and significance of what is being sacrificed in the desperate quest to raise scores has not been inside a school lately (46). (Author's Note: This quip is confirmed by this author's recent visits to many elementary, middle, and high schools.)

8. *Many educators are leaving the field because of what is being done to schools in the name of accountability and tougher standards.*

Kohn points out that the *New York Times* reported in its lead story of September 3, 2000, that "A growing number of schools are rudderless, struggling to replace a graying core of principals at a time when the pressure to raise test scores and other new demands have made an already significant job an increasingly thankless one" (46).

Kohn summarizes this rather telling commentary by noting that "Prospective teachers are rethinking whether they want to begin a career in which high test scores matter most, and in which they will be pressured to produce these scores" (47).

Another commentary by a prominent figure, Robert B. Reich, former secretary of labor who is currently a university professor of social and economic policy at Brandeis University in Waltham, Massachusetts, echoes Kohn's sentiments and broadens the argument to include key economic concerns surrounding the frenzy of standardized testing. Reich notes that "The latest rage in education is standardized tests" (2001, 64). He points out that "We're embracing standardized tests just when the new economy is eliminating standardized jobs" (64). The previous remark about the new economy should be obvious to anybody who has been around the job market for the past ten years with all its vicissitudes and unpredictable change. However, very few take Reich's comments seriously. Perhaps the reason is that most of us do not want to face the undeniable fact that standardized testing is perhaps the least important part of schools. Likewise, it is probably the least significant indicator of how schools perform.

Reich notes that

> Most people spent most of their working lives performing the same operations over and over, in the company of any other people who perform the same or similar operations. A standardized education was (used to be) appropriate because jobs were standardized. In general, the largest pedagogical challenge was to train young people to sit still for long periods of time, be patient, follow directions, and be punctual. These were the core competencies that industry required. (64, 48)

His commentary rightfully includes remarks about the differences required in the new economy in terms of being successful in a job. For example, he notes that "Many of the new jobs depend on creativity—on out-of-the-box thinking, originality, and flair. Almost by definition, standardized tests can't measure these sorts of things" (48).

The useful comparison can be obtained by comparing the MCAS (Massachusetts Comprehensive Assessment System) grade 4 mathematics results against the NAEP (National Assessment of Educational Progress) mathematics results in the same year. This author has obtained results for both exams directly from the sponsoring organizations: Massachusetts Department of Education and National Center for Education Statistics. In the year 2000, the most recent year for which this kind of comparison can be made, it can be noted that the category deemed "proficient" exists for both testing instruments. The comparison may or may not be completely valid; however, the fact of the matter is that the description given by each test for what *proficient* means is very similar: in the case of MCAS, *proficient* means that the student "shows solid understanding of challenging subject matter and is able to solve a wide variety of problems"; in the case of the NAEP, *proficient* means "solid academic performance for each grade assessed." Let us now examine the results in the year 2000.

Twenty-eight percent of fourth graders who took the MCAS mathematics test scored in the proficient range. For NAEP the result in the year 2000 revealed that 23% scored in the proficient range on the mathematics test. In contrast, the category of "needs improvement" on the MCAS is defined as "shows partial understanding of subject matter," whereas in the case of the comparable NAEP category (called "basic"), the analogous category is similarly defined as "denoting partial mastery of prerequisite knowledge and skills." For the MCAS 42% ended up scoring in the needs improvement category, while for NAEP 43% were deemed at the basic level. We could continue these kinds of comparisons to demonstrate the similar result of these two high-stakes tests, yet it would be foolhardy to do so since we would know instinctively that the students who performed poorly on the MCAS in Massachusetts in mathematics would be a microcosm of the performance of the entire country on the same subject matter as represented in the results of the NAEP mathematics test. What does this mean?

While it is of course impossible to equate fully two separate mathematics tests, that is, the MCAS versus the NAEP results in grade 4, we could speculate or infer that these tests were measuring mastery of similar kinds of subject matter content. To make this argument stronger, an examination of grade 8, for example, demonstrates a similar performance between the MCAS and the NAEP. Once again, the percentages are comparable with 22% of eighth graders scoring in the proficient range on the NAEP and 27% scoring in the proficient range on the MCAS assessment. Thirty-eight percent ended up in the basic range on the NAEP mathematics tests while 27% needed improvement on the MCAS mathematics portion. It is interesting to note these similarities, but it may be even more interesting to infer from these results that *important concepts in mathematics are not being learned well by enough students in the public schools of this country*. Furthermore, the results get worse as one goes up in the grades.

The failure rates on the MCAS from grade 4 to grade 8 in mathematics show a significant jump (18% to 39%) in the year 2000, while a more gradual increase is noted on the results of the NAEP mathematics assessment in the year 2000, that is, from 31% to 34%. Much speculation has been offered in order to explain why such large numbers of youngsters perform so poorly in mathematics. It is not the intention of this author to explore that question at this time. Rather, we need to ask ourselves whether we can (1) rely on these results; and (2) depend on the implication of the results to guide our future actions. We might look to the curriculum for some guidance as to what has transpired over the years in mathematics teaching.

As David Labaree informs us, "The system has a genius for incorporating curriculum change without fundamental organization" (*Lessons of a Century*, 2000, 148). Labaree's criticism is relevant to our discussion of mathematics. He says that "The failure of curriculum reform was certainly not the result of a lack of effort. At various times during the last 100 years, reformers have issued high visibility reports proposing dramatic changes in the curriculum (*The Cardinal Principles of Secondary Education* in 1918, a *Nation at Risk* in 1983); created whole new subject areas (Social Studies, vocational education, special education); sought to reorganize the curriculum around a variety of new principles (ability grouping, the project method, life adjustment, back to basics, inclusion, critical thinking); and launched movements to reinvent particular subjects" (*Lessons of a Century*, 148).

It goes without saying that the failure of curriculum reform to improve the achievement level of students is matched only by the discriminatory aspects of the curriculum when viewed against achievement levels by ethnicity. Black and Hispanic students fail at much higher rates than do white students (Massachusetts Department of Education and National Center for Education Statistics). Not only is this statement true in the year 2000, but it is a pattern that has existed at least since the late 1980s and continues to this day. Gary W. Phillips, Deputy Commissioner at the National Center for Education Statistics, further accentuates this point when he says that "gaps persist in academic performance and educational participation among different racial/ethnic groups, socioeconomic groups, and school sectors. The gaps between the average reading scores of white students and black students ages 9, 13, and 17 have remained stable or increased since the late 1980s. In mathematics, high poverty levels in schools are associated with low student achievement in the fourth grade. While the percentages of drop-outs in the population of white young adults and black young adults have declined, the percentage for Hispanics has remained higher than that of other groups and remains high. Finally, private school students in general scored higher than public school students in reading, mathematics, and science" (Phillips, 2002, ix).

Lest we have any doubt about which factors matter most in terms of producing these kinds of failures in academic subjects, it has been demonstrated that high levels of poverty produce lower scores in grade 4 mathematics (Phillips, 2002, 58). Whether we view these results as the product of a failure of curriculum reform or as a failure of the entire teaching profession, there is little doubt that factors such as socioeconomic status or parental involvement weigh heavily in the achievement outcomes of all students. As a matter of fact, it could be argued that the test results from all standardized tests across the country as reported in chapter 1 have served to confuse the American public and focus attention away from key factors that most reasonable people agree count more in the actual outcome of schooling (factors such as socioeconomic status, race, ethnicity, and so forth, all of which seem to matter more than curriculum reform and teaching effectiveness in terms of the eventual success or failure of students in any given school).

Organizational psychology provides us with ample evidence that the "true score" on any test is a reflection of a variety of input variables and has a range of possible scores that reflects (1) the notion of SEM (Standard Error of Measurement) *plus* all other factors that have been previously mentioned in this chapter, namely race, ethnicity, socioeconomic status, and parental involvement. Let us now introduce the notion of intelligence as an additional significant factor that will, of course, impact the size of the range of possible scores as well as the potential for future learning on the part of any individual.

In terms of change theory, it is important to note that there are several principles of school change that emerge from an analysis of total quality thinking (personal synthesis of research on TQ-total quality). For example, it is generally recognized that school change occurs because of a preconceived planning process, that is, change in educational setting is infrequently random. A second principle advises that it is through teachers that lasting change occurs. This is particularly noteworthy since it is the premise of this book that there has been mostly a top-down kind of approach to reforming education in the United States over the past ten or fifteen years. We know that lasting change requires a bottom-up approach or at least the active involvement of teachers in real classrooms.

A third principle to take into account is that school change must explicitly target student performance. This means that most of the discussion in education reform ought to be about improving the lives of students and not about governance, curriculum, frameworks, and testing, as we have seen in chapters 1 and 2. The idea is that if the change cannot be linked to improved student performance, then it is not worth making. A fourth principle is that we need to reconceive the workplace to match a twenty-first-century culture. For example, it is particularly noteworthy that schools have continued to be set up, organized, and operated almost exactly as they were seventy years ago. This is a disturbing aspect of education reform since, as we have seen, education reform legislation tends to repeat the mistakes of the past.

A fifth principle is that we ought to build on practices that have proven to increase student achievement. Now it must be noted that there are very few practices that have been conclusively documented to demonstrate this, and for that reason we do not have a very strong foundational base upon which to build. It will be the main focus in chapter 6 to consider *instruction* and to decide what kinds of practices are most suitable for schools in the twenty-first century.

A sixth principle is that schools need not only to be accountable but also rewarded for improved student performance. They need to be objectively evaluated, and if agreed upon changes do not lead to increased student achievement, then it is incumbent upon everyone to consider a reorganization of a particular school. (*Author's Note:* It is not the intention of this author to confuse the matter of whether the typical data generated to assess student achievement are worthwhile in terms of capturing the essence of what goes on in schools. Indeed, any teacher will say that thinking about educational outcome in these terms is misguided and unreflective of teaching and learning.) What needs to be emphasized here is that the literature on total quality has always acknowledged that *accountability* is a key to any change effort. What we must work on and accomplish in the very near future is a methodology to decide how to know if schools succeed. (This matter will be taken up in more detail in chapter 9.)

The seventh and eighth principles that can be identified (personal synthesis of literature on total quality) are *lasting change takes time* and *change is a process not an event*. Indeed, the fastest way to accomplish change is to give teachers and students enough time to make meaningful and lasting change within the classroom environment. Also, since change is a process, it must be acknowledged that no short-term, quick-fix approaches to improvement will take hold and, in fact, improve the quality of teaching and learning in schools.

THE DIMINISHED RETURNS OF STANDARDIZED TEST DATA

Hugh Price, president of the National Urban League in New York City, recently commented that "Youngsters who can barely read by the fourth grade face a steep uphill climb the rest of the way through school and later in life" (2001, 48). Now we have seen in this chapter that Black and Hispanic children (we could also have added American Indian children) are not achieving academically up to speed. They lag way behind where they should be in terms of achievement level in math and reading and in other academic subjects. The data that we have used are precisely those that politicians and policymakers have identified as the metric that we should use to know whether a school succeeds. (Of course, the premise of this author is that this is misguided.) We should know by now that the achievement levels that lag behind are not going to catch up. In fact, as Price notes, we can expect from fourth grade on that the achievement levels will get worse and indeed an analysis of all data from the National Center for Education Statistics (*The Condition of Education,* 2002) indicates that minority children perform less well than their white counterparts and continue to lose ground over the eight years of education from grade 4 to graduation (personal analysis of NCES report, 2002). Moreover, Price's analysis goes beyond a mere reporting of this achievement gap between minority children and white children and elucidates other important problems inherent in this gap:

> I believe it's time to pause for problem identification and adjust our sights. When you think about it, there actually are several achievement gaps. Beyond the stark racial disparities revealed by NAEP, there is a gap between how American children in general and low-performing minority students in particular stack up against children in the rest of the world. There's the unsettling claim by some experts that a pupil who earns an A in an inner city school knows about as much in a given subject as a suburbanite who earns a C. Nor is the achievement gap confined to inner city and rural schools. Middle-class Black students in integrated suburban schools generally lag behind their white and Asian-American classmates. (48)

Price's analysis is all the more disconcerting and troublesome when we consider the long-term effects of this gap. One of the more obvious repercussions has to do with economics. Clearly, students who do not do well in school are unlikely to be successful in the workplace and are unlikely to be able to achieve a quality of life that we typically ascribe to living in a democratic society. Price's pointed analysis is as follows: the cumulative effect of the preparation gap is the economic apartheid that produces higher unemployment rates and lower household incomes for some groups in our society (34).

This still leaves us with somewhat of a dilemma concerning student achievement and concerning the long-term effects of not achieving in school. We have seen that change theory offers us insights as to how the organization itself might deal with achievement gaps. We have also seen that student ability must factor into this equation, yet it is unclear as to how to measure this particular feature of the problem of achievement. A third factor ought to be introduced at this time, and it is precisely that *family background* is an inescapably profound influence on eventual achievement in schools. Indeed, John E. Chubb and Terry M. Moe, in a groundbreaking work that relates the effect of schooling on the eventual economic condition of the country, demonstrate that these three variables (namely ability, organization, and family background) are, in fact, the three major causes of student achievement (1990, 140). They further state that "All things being equal, a student in an effectively organized school should achieve at least a half year more than a student in an ineffectively organized school over the last two years of high school" (140). They go on to say that this kind of effect is a substantial one and, indeed, very important to the whole picture of how schooling and the marketplace interrelate. While Chubb and Moe made a significant contribution to this argument well over a decade ago (*and prior to the start of a decade of education reform legislation*), they nonetheless fell into the trap, in this author's opinion, of putting too much emphasis on the data that would lead one to make these conclusions. The reductionist conclusion of a half year more of achievement in school is problematic at best and overly simplistic at worse.

The AERA (American Educational Research Association) took a stand, a little more than a decade after Moe and Chubb's work, on the matter of testing and, in particular, on what is now commonly known as "high-stakes testing" in pre-K–12 education. It is this association's position that every high-stakes achievement testing program in education should meet all of the following conditions ("Position Statement" 2000, 24–25.)

1. *Protection against high-stakes decisions based on a single test*
There is credible evidence that a test score may not adequately reflect a student's true proficiency and alternative acceptable means should be provided by which to demonstrate attainment of the tested standards.

2. *Adequate resources and opportunity to learn*
It is the belief of the association that students must have had a meaningful opportunity to learn the tested content and cognitive processes.

3. *Validation of each separate intended use*
This is a very important condition since it reflects the growing unrest among many educators and researchers about the validity, or lack thereof, of many high-stakes tests. Tests that are valid for one use may be invalid for another, and each separate use of a high-stakes test for various purposes requires a separate evaluation of the strengths and limitations of the testing program and the test itself.

4. *Full disclosure of likely negative consequences of high-stakes testing programs*

Where credible scientific evidence suggests that a given type of testing program is likely to have negative side effects, test developers and users should make a serious effort to explain these possible effects to policymakers.

5. *Alignment between the test and the curriculum*

This should no longer be a problematic or debatable area. Yet we find that there is frequently a lack of alignment between a test and the curriculum it supposedly measures. One solution offered by the association is that multiple test forms should be used or new test forms should be introduced on a regular basis in order to avoid a narrowing of the curriculum toward just the content sampled on a particular form.

6. *Validity of passing scores and achievement levels*

When testing programs use specific scores to determine "passing" or to define reporting categories such as "proficient," the validity of these specific scores must be established in addition to demonstrating the representativeness of the test content. (*Author's Note:* We have seen in chapter 2 that another problem arises concerning the definition of minimal competency, that is, the fact that the minimal level set for competency is always the least successful accomplishment on the test.)

7. *Opportunities for meaningful remediation for examinees who fail high-stakes tests*

We should acknowledge the accomplishment in this area of many states that offer remediation programs for students who do not pass high-stakes tests; however, there is no effort to remediate the weaknesses of the student's academic profile except to teach the student how to answer correctly the questions that he or she did not answer correctly on a test the first time around. In other words, teaching to the test becomes the exclusive art and science of the remediation session.

8. *Appropriate attention to language differences among examinees*

One of the most controversial areas when discussing high-stakes tests is the language proficiency of many students who do not speak English as their primary language. If English language learners are tested in English, their performance should be interpreted in the light of their language proficiency. This is not frequently done nor are special accommodations for limited English language learners usually provided.

9. *Appropriate attention to students with disabilities*
This is a self-explanatory category and steps should be taken at all times to ensure that tests accurately reflect the intended construct and not reflect disabilities extraneous to the intention of the measurement.

10. *Careful adherence to explicit rules for determining which students are to be tested*
This is a controversial area since the number of disabled students and LEP students (limited English proficient) is a growing concern among those who are monitoring the use of high-stakes test results. This area will need careful attention.

11. *Sufficient reliability for each intended use*
Needless to say, there is very little reliability in the scores. As we have seen, this reductionist approach to assessing achievement of students or accomplishment of schools has never been demonstrated to be reliable in all cases or for each intended use.

12. *Ongoing evaluation of intended and unintended effects of high-stakes testing*
With any high-stakes testing program, ongoing evaluation of both intended and unintended consequences is essential. In most cases, the governmental body that mandates the test should also provide resources for a continuing program of research and for dissemination of research findings concerning both the positive and the negative effects of the testing program.

Thus the would-be policymakers and education reformers must be in the wrong race. There really is no winning here since the statistical analysis that is frequently used to report the results of standardized tests (namely results reported as standard deviation, deviation from the mean, percentile rank, or other similar statistical devices) do not inform us, in any meaningful way, about the domain level knowledge of students and do not help us to devise programs and experiences to match students' needs, both educational and social. In fact, one could argue that the real crisis in education has more to do with the quality of life among our students than it does with the so-called lack of skills or achievement of students in school.

The psychologist Robert Evans, who consults with school districts in Massachusetts and is the author of *The Human Side of School Change* (2002), takes the argument even further when he claims that "The truth is, America doesn't have a crisis in schooling. It has something much worse: a crisis in child-rearing" (2002a, 48). He goes on to say something that we would do well to heed and to take seriously as we ponder the next decade of reform in the United States:

> What has deteriorated most over 30 years is not the skills of our teachers but the lives of our students. The supports vital to good development (and hence to schooling) are in free fall. The symptoms of the crisis—a continuing deterioration and the academic achievement, work ethic, and civility of many of our young people—appear vividly at school, but they begin well before it and extend well beyond it. Schools, in fact, are victims of the crisis more than its perpetrators. They can never overcome fundamental problems that start at home. (2002a, 48, 37)

It is certainly easy and comfortable to echo Evans's remarks and even confirm what we should all know by now: that the family is at the heart of learning and that children who are well cared for and feel secure function better at school and achieve a more fulfilling life than those who are not. When parents encourage self-regulation and perseverance, when they limit television, monitor homework, and ensure regular school attendance, children's lives improve (and test scores generally go up). No, there is no evidence hard and fast that would prove these remarks, nor has this author given in to the reductionist environment that has pervaded the education reform movement. But let us be serious. We know that we have an enormous problem, and we also know that we are far from the solution. It is time to take this problem and explore it in a different way. (This matter will be taken up fully in chapters 8 and 9.) But, for the moment, let us take seriously Evans's conclusion which is, at the same time, chilling and incisive: "At the ordinary end of today's spectrum, students are more difficult to reach and teach, their concentration and perseverance more fragile, and their language and behavior more provocative. At the catastrophic end lie the Columbines" (2002a, 37).

CONCLUSION

Arthur Levine, president of Teachers College, Columbia University, comes to a stark conclusion in a 2001 commentary when, in his concluding remarks, he points to an "endgame for school reform." First, Levine says that we must get beyond sharp ideological divisions. Second, he talks about the remarkable job we have done in upgrading our suburban schools, but he points to the fact that we have not made comparable improvements in urban schools and, in fact, we have largely failed. Third, he sees a need to do a better job of educating teachers and school administrators and principals and superintendents. He sees too many weak preparatory programs, which too often train *managers* not the *educational leaders* schools so badly need today. Levine further states that it is time for the states to close poor programs, strengthen weak programs, and support strong ones (52). His summative evaluation of what the alternative is to not heeding his three-part plan is as follows: "[W]hat we will have to show for 20 years of hard work are a sea of reports documenting a crisis and proposed remedies, a cornucopia of innovations that were attempted under the banner of reform, anecdotes about why each was successful, and an education system that better serves our most advantaged young people. We need to do better" (52). I believe that we have already attained the summary evaluation that Levine states as an alternative to following his advice about education reform. Moreover, I believe that this so-called endgame for school reform, that is, that school reform will not be the showcase news item that it currently is, will probably be true sooner than we think.

It is the belief of this author that we will begin to correct the tremendous setbacks in education, which have occurred over the past twenty years, only by focusing our attention on the broadest possible conceptualization of curriculum, instruction, and assessment. To move beyond clichés in these areas is not an easy task. It seems as if everything has already been said about curriculum theory and design, about instructional strategies and methodologies, and about assessment of student learning through authentic and alternative means. Truth be told, we have not even begun to access the best thinking in these three areas. So what is left to be done?

My own platform for avoiding the inevitably dark and fruitless race to show achievement gains is to stop the senseless frenzy of testing that has taken hold in the United States since the federal government issued the 1983 "A Nation at Risk" report. Even if we could win the race, what would it prove? If we have students who can pass a test, will this in any way mean that the quality of life will improve? (I believe we all think it needs to improve.) I am concerned, deeply concerned, that not only is the race to show achievement gains not winnable but the conceptualization of such a race speaks to a flaw in American education and a serious defect in the delivery of sound curriculum, instruction, and assessment within the schools. It must be viewed as ludicrous to try to compare school districts one to the other or to compare the fifty states on the basis of test scores. Let us remind ourselves that there are only three known testing programs that are administered *in every state*: the SAT (college admission test), the ACT (also a college admission test), and the NAEP (the progress report of the fifty states in key academic subjects). Are we so confident in the reliability, validity, and comprehensiveness of these three tests such that we will make major educational decisions for a whole generation of children and young adults based on the data? Indeed, this is a rhetorical question. We nonetheless must take seriously the pervasive reductionist mentality that is dominating American life at this time.

CHAPTER 4

SEMANTICS OF EDUCATION REFORM
Words and Concepts Devoid of Meaning

AS WE SAW IN CHAPTER 3, it is difficult, if not impossible, to find results on record anywhere, or at any time, that can even remotely celebrate an accomplishment of schooling that can be clearly traced to an education reform law or act implemented in the past decade. This reality, that is, persistent failure in schools, is a statement of educational failure at the policy level not at the school level. First and foremost, the problem begins with the persistent focus of state legislatures on the concept of governance as a target for reform efforts. What this means is that the legislation that has been enacted over the past decade has mostly concerned itself, first and foremost, with laws that address the problem of governance in schools. Therefore, education reform acts have typically addressed the powers inherent in school committees versus those of superintendents versus those of principals, and so forth. In other words, all of the effort and energy have gone into reconnecting how schools are run. And to make matters worse, teachers are rarely, if ever, consulted about how to fix the problems that we believe exist in schools.

Now it should be noted early on that *there are problems.* However, to conceive the problem as being entwined in the governance structure of the schools or school districts is, in my opinion, an ill-defined problem. I would have to say experientially that, if anything, governance of schools as an issue does little or nothing to change the nature of the teaching and learning that goes on in classrooms. Yes, we would all want to believe that there is a great deal of supervision and evaluation of teachers by principals or other supervisors. The reality is that the number of administrators available to supervise teachers is so small that there is, at best, cursory observation of teaching.

FAILURE AT THE POLICY LEVEL

We know that all education reform efforts have begun at the top of the educational hierarchy and have worked their way down to the classroom. It is no surprise, therefore, that children in schools receive very little benefit from the activity that goes on at the top of the hierarchy. There is, of course, no mystery about how this works (Apple, 1982; Sergiovanni, 1995). The unfortunate reality for children is that it has been well known for at least thirty years now that the top-down approach to administering schools and curriculum is the least effective way to get results at the grassroots level, namely in the classrooms (Sarasin, 1990). There are better ways to establish positive learning environments (Senge, 1994).

As noted earlier, teachers are rarely asked their opinion on how to reform education. There is this persistent belief that teachers must be part of the problem, that they must be too disinterested in their own profession to offer reasonable and intelligent solutions. How ludicrous. The idea that the very practitioner of teaching and learning, namely the teacher, would be unable to articulate what the problem is defies logic and common sense. This should not surprise us at all. What is more, policymakers and legislators persist in devising elaborate schemes of reform that involve typically the curriculum and testing so as to try to improve the actual learning outcomes of schooling.

As we will see in chapter 5, which deals with curriculum, a very unfortunate principle that has continued to guide education reform is the following: that what is learned in schools has been taught there. What we will see in chapter 5 is that standardized tests are measuring a far greater array of knowledge than what is taught in schools. Furthermore, we will know that the tests themselves are measuring something more than just the daily activities of children in schools.

In terms of curriculum and testing—since these are the second and third most common targets of reform efforts—policymakers have found that the easiest way to deal with something as elusive and complex as "curriculum" (that is, knowledge) is to construct very discrete and orderly frameworks to guide the curriculum that is taught in schools. Once these frameworks are established, tests are developed, piloted, field-tested, and (sometimes) validated, and the results of these activities end up producing a lot of data and allowing policymakers to gauge metrically the improvement of schools.

All of this really boils down to a massive lack of correct definition of the problem, which for teachers at least, if there is a problem at all, resides in the domain of salary, class size, administrative support, and parental involvement. Thus we have a very troubling dichotomy between the teacher, who is excluded from policymaking, and the policymaker/legislator, who devises governance, curriculum, and testing schemes to try to improve the schools without the consensus and agreement of the very person who is in charge of curriculum delivery.

In the next section we will take a look at linguistic theory so we can get some kind of an idea about the lexicon and the concenptualization mechanisms that are used by policymakers to convince the public of the rightfulness of their education reform packages.

LINGUISTICS IN ACTION: MORPHOLOGY, PHONOLOGY, SYNTAX, AND SEMANTICS

To shed light on this matter, let us examine a very telling observation by Heather C. Hill (2001).

> My observations suggest a further complication, one that falls at the meeting-place of policy and . . . cognition: language. Standards exist at a level above actual classroom practice and thus are limited in the picture they can paint of subject matter and instruction, leaving locals a tremendous interpretive task. Furthermore, the specific words that comprise state standards often hold specialized meanings within reform and local communities, and these meanings often do not meet. State curriculum writers crafted their product using words such as "explore," "construct," and "understand" to signify certain expectations about student learning, and terms like "discrete math" or "algebra" to signify mathematical content to which they wanted children exposed. Yet locals, for the most part, did not have access to the reform communities that supplied particular meanings for those words. Instead, when curriculum committee members encountered these words, they understood and used them based on definitions supplied by more local subject matter communities, including some conventional student curriculum materials and the professional development that

accompanied it. In doing so, they often missed the instructional reforms state policymakers meant to imply. (290–91)

Hill's study at the University of Michigan on this issue of policy and the language that is particular to it sheds substantial light on the argument we are exploring in this chapter. While language is taken for granted as the vehicle that will be used to effect actual changes in achievement outcomes of schools, this assumption has yet to have proven itself either useful or valid. We see in Hill's work that not only is there potential for a mismatch between teacher and policymaker but also, even worse, that there is always a mismatch between the local community and the policymakers. What this presents to us is a rather thorny educational problem framed within a field at least as old as knowledge and perhaps older, namely linguistics. Let us examine linguistics to see if we can figure out why these words do not carry the meanings they intend from top to bottom, from policymaker to classroom.

Linguistics is made up minimally of four parts: morphology, phonology, syntax, and semantics. These four parts have specific meaning and relevance to our argument about the semantics of education reform. Let us consider each one in turn.

Morphology

Morphology is, simply stated, the smallest meaning unit of any given word. We all know and understand the meaning and function of the prefix "re-" as in the word *repaint*. We understand this prefix to signal that the action should be done again. Likewise, we understand the suffix "-ful" to mean "plenty," as in *insightful*. These meaning units do not have any ambiguity. However, the words that are frequently used to describe and effect educational change do not have as clear a meaning.

For example, consider the words that Hill mentions in her observation above (words such as "explore," "construct," and "understand"). In everyday usage there is no ambiguity in using these words because the speaker using them does not intend or care about the specificity of the action that might come after using these words. When a mother says, "Why don't you just go up in your room and explore the topic of zoology on the Internet," the child understands that it involves looking at some of the related materials about animals that can be found on his or her computer. Yet never is it the case that the mother intends the child to explore in very specific ways or to follow certain steps to attain a goal. Rather, *explore* here has a more generalized meaning that is understood between the mother and the child. Indeed, the word *understand* can be clear when in conversation one person

Semantics of Education Reform　　　　　　　　　　　　　　　　　　　　59

will say to another, "I understand that." Does this mean that the person saying it really grasps all of the detail of the subject about which the other person was talking? Hardly. We know that will rarely be the case or that it will be checked by the original speaker in the conversation.

Hill mentions mathematics and terms such as "discrete math" and "algebra," yet there is a wide range of levels of study of these subjects. Thus to inquire about the availability of studying algebra within a school would not give the person inquiring a clear understanding of what the curriculum in that course is going to look like. In other words, all of these words are, in some sense, general enough to be used effectively in daily conversation, yet they lack the kind of specificity when used in policy matters to effect the kind of improvement in schools that is mandated by the education reform laws.

Phonology

The phonology of policymaking is less of a problem since phonology refers to the sound system of a language. Typically, the issue of phonology will involve intonation and perhaps emphasis, and, therefore, it is usually the case that phonology shows up, at least in the case of education reform, as an example of politics, pure and simple. In other words, policymakers will benefit or not benefit from the art and science of phonology. The sounds of the language offer all of that (intonation and emphasis) and phonology interfaces with the meaning units embodied in the concept of morphology by taking the written word, the analytical word, and putting it into holistic utterances that then convey a full and holistic meaning that the speaker intends to convey. Policymakers hope that their education plans and acts and legislations have these kinds of holistic and clear meanings. However, they almost never do. As we saw previously, the meaning units that are conveyed easily among people in daily life do not convey easily at all when they are written into legal documents, including legislative acts.

As Hill points out, "Words have no inherent meaning. Instead, they signify ideas or actions ascribed to them by communities, whether those communities are speakers of the language, workers in a technical field, or children on a playground" (303).

She makes an eloquent argument about meaning when she says:

> Oftentimes, one word holds different meanings for different communities, as when the word "variance" means one thing to lawyers (discrepancies in statements during a proceeding), another to statisticians (the square of the standard deviation), and still another to the general population (the difference between what occurs and what's expected, or a reprieve from local zoning regulations).

How one interprets this word depends on not only the context in which one finds it, but also upon what communities of meaning the reader or user has access to. (Schwab, 1978; Bakhtin, 1981; both in Hill, 2001, 303)

Another example of ambiguity, indeed confusion, which arises in language use involves the field of mathematics. Hill aptly points out in her conclusion that "One practical result of the policy trickle down process is that state mathematics standards may lose much of their potential even before being passed along to teachers in the form of instructional guidance" (313).

Syntax

The notion of syntax involves of course nothing more than word order. Syntax is particular to each language group, and the Romance group of five languages (French, Italian, and so forth) has a syntax that is distinguishably different from the Germanic group (which includes German and English and others). Syntax presents very little of a problem when we talk of policymaking except that the way in which legislative acts are worded sometimes causes confusion simply because of the length of sentences that thereby cloud and confound the word orders, that is, which words belong to which other words in the law in order to make sense of the entire law. For our purposes there is not much else to say about syntax except that it is a key functional notion within the field of linguistics, and we should keep in mind that written laws tend to be obtuse and therefore have a great capacity to distort syntax.

Finally, what I consider the most important area to look at is semantics. Let us give this particular topic a very close examination. In the next section I will talk about how the framing of the so-called problem of improving schools is wrapped up in the notion of meanings and the semantic structure of sentences.

Semantics

As an aficionado of linguistics during my graduate work at Boston University, I frequently spent free time pouring through any and all books that I could get my hands on dealing with any branch of linguistics. I found particularly fascinating areas such as anthropology, psychology, and sociology, all three of which intersect nicely with the field itself. Of course the philosophy of language was of particular interest since it offered very unique explanations about how and why we go about using language at all.

Let us start by addressing the issue of the dictionary. We all know that there are dictionaries that provide a reference for us when we need to look up a technical word or a word unfamiliar to us. In contrast, we have all learned the grammatical rules of our own language and all its essentials by the age of five or so, and from then on we continue the process of acquiring the vocabulary, and new uses, throughout our lives. The store of lexical items that we draw upon for our own linguistic interactions with others tends to be embodied by a set of lexical items familiar enough to us that we use these terms with nuance and with finesse. Indeed, many times words or lexical items help define one's personality. This is quite different from the kinds of language (sets of words) that tend to be used within legislative acts.

In his 1965 groundbreaking work, Noam Chomsky points out that there is a deep semantic structure of every sentence and that it would be possible to relate, through transformational rules, the semantic representation (or deep structure) to a surface structure that would get phonological representation in an utterance. He further demonstrated that it is possible to argue that syntactic representations could be derived from a semantic base *or* that a semantic representation could be derived from a syntactic base. In other words, there is a bi-directionality in conveying meaning and that meaning is dependent upon the intention of the speaker coupled with a correct syntactic and/or semantic usage of a particular sentence of a particular language.

In fact, Jeffrey Leech, in *Semantics*, argues that the study of presupposition cannot be properly separated from the semantic representations of an utterance (361). Therefore, a presupposition (which takes the form of an incomplete sentence or a relative clause) will be embedded in many of the policies that are written to reform education. Unfortunately, presuppositions that are obvious in everyday speech (for example, saying that the orphan's father drinks heavily presupposes that the orphan has a father) will not be as obvious in the legalistic jargon so typical of an educational policy.

All of this brings up the following relevant question: Is it the case that the language of educational policy, and specifically the language of education reform policy, is so misunderstood and misapplied that it, by itself, explains the reason for the continued failure in schools? I think the answer is clearly that it is not the whole answer to the question of educational failure.

The difficulty in any attempt to analyze education reform is that the incipient motivation to perform such elaborate legislation, effort, and expenditure of money is never clear. We are told repeatedly in the media that schools have failed or are failing children. This notion is reinforced by education officials at the state level who, as politicians, take this kind of an analysis and transform it into action. Now the only action that education officials can take, which will hopefully impact the schools, is to legislate tangible activities that the officials hope will begin to alleviate the problem.

Now the problem is, as we have seen previously, ill defined. This author pointed out earlier that governance, curriculum, and testing become the tangible objects one can manipulate. We further saw that these particular objects, once manipulated, do not necessarily translate into improvement of learning outcomes. All of our reasons for this have resided, first of all, in a wide-ranging effort across the country to show some achievement gains so that the public will be mollified and more likely to support future political action on the part of the legislators.

Semantics and other linguistic notions offer some explanation as to why the legislative acts may not have worked their way into the actual classrooms, but our picture is still quite incomplete. Two problems persist: (1) we still have not identified the problem; and (2) once we do this we still do not know exactly what the reform of education really means. This topic is the focus of the next two sections.

THE PROBLEM

It should be clear by now that the major focus of this chapter on education reform is linguistic analysis applied to the formulation of policy at the state level in order to divine exactly what the problem is that we are trying to reform or solve. In this chapter we are guided by the notion that reform as a concept seems to be devoid of meaning. While there are, perhaps, well-intentioned formulations of policy to *correct* what is perceived as a failure on the part of schools, we have seen that, in fact, the problem must be much more complex than simply residing within schools or, put another way, that the problem is beyond simply reforming the governance of schools, reforming the curriculum of schools, and reforming the testing procedures of schools. Let us now consider what the problem really is.

In this author's estimation, the mismatch between what teachers believe is the problem (namely salary, class size, and support from parents and administrators) and what policymakers believe is the problem (namely governance, curriculum, and testing) creates an environment in which a lot of time, money, and effort are expended on the wrong issues. If we hypothesize that the wording and concepts embodied in legislative acts of education reform are, in fact, devoid of much meaning or, let us say, devoid of a shared meaning between teachers and policymakers, then it is not too difficult to conclude that the results of statewide education reform will most likely not correct any actual problem but, in fact, will solve only the problems formulated by the policy itself, namely governance, curriculum, and testing.

Semantics of Education Reform

Now we have seen that education reform acts (Massachusetts was given as an example in chapter 2) have, in fact, reformed the governance structure of schools in at least one state. In fact, we have seen in chapter 1 that this pattern of addressing governance, curriculum, and testing as the sole focus of reform shows up over and over again.

The difficulty in defining the problem further exacerbates the question of what reform really means. Reform ought to mean that we are correcting a real problem that impacts students' lives. The conceptualization of this kind of problem, it is not inconceivable to postulate, must reside within the actual interaction in a classroom among students and between students and the teacher. Since most of the time in school is spent interacting with other students and with a teacher or teachers, then it is not difficult to realize that reform of education must include this level. This author has designed a linguistic model that attempts to locate the most meaningful point of delivery within the educational enterprise. This point of delivery has been defined as the actual teaching act (that is, when curriculum is delivered to students in a lesson in schools). Let us now take a look at the main features of this particular design. (See Figure 4.1)

Simply stated, the model demonstrates that what happens in a classroom, in the communication between teacher and student(s), is subject to extensive miscommunication caused in part by the fact that linguistic meaning, during the act of encoding/decoding, loses some of its component parts (codes). Thus the model suggests that resolution of the miscommunication must, by definition, occur after the instruction (that is, the teacher's lesson) has ended. Furthermore, this process (that is, resolving) is most appropriately activated by the teacher, who usually occupies the most critical, central role in teaching and learning.

WHAT DOES REFORM REALLY MEAN?

The question of what reform really means can only be answered if we recall that there is a lack of agreement on which elements within the educational system need reform. As noted several times previously in this book, there is a serious disconnect between what policymakers believe the problem is and what teachers understand the problem to be. The linguistic model that is demonstrated in this chapter shows this author's belief that the only area upon which to focus reform efforts would be the actual delivery of curriculum. The actual delivery of curriculum is the only place where we can be sure that some kind of teaching is performed within a school.

FIGURE 4.1

PSYCHOLINGUISTIC MODEL OF KNOWLEDGE ACQUISITION: A MODEL OF NON-EQUIVALENCY IN FORMS OF KNOWLEDGE SHARED IN LEARNING ENVIRONMENTS

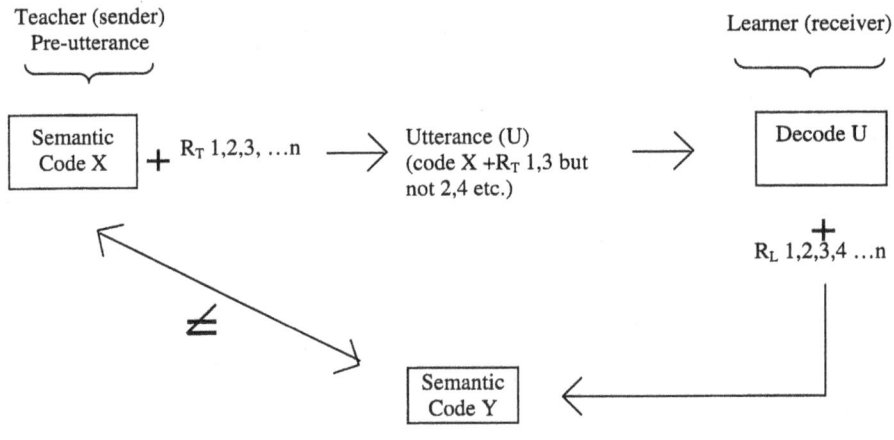

Thus, resolution window needed here in post-instruction stage

R = a unified set of code relationships
☐ = IKB (Individual Knowledge Base)

[Explanation of how encoded in Individual Knowledge Base (IKB) of Learner]
Semantic Code Y is the utterance, as "heard" by the learner, plus R_T 1,3 but not 2,4 since they (2,4, etc.) remained at pre-utterance stage

One thing is clear, and that is that the conundrum we call failure in schools is not an area that will be reformed at the highest level of the educational enterprise. We must focus effort at the actual delivery of curriculum level if we really want to impact what students learn and what they understand their world to be about. The hostile environment within the educational system today is largely due to this so-called lack of agreement on what reform really means. As we saw previously in this chapter, the mismatch between teachers and policymakers continues to present itself as a major obstacle to improvement of teaching and learning.

WHAT WE KNOW FROM SOUND THEORY

Jerome Bruner in his classic work *The Process of Education* notes that the delivery of curriculum within schools ought to be conducted in a spiral fashion (1960). And since we know from the years following Bruner's classic work on education that thinking has become a prime focus of school improvement activities, we need to take seriously his words in the introduction to Lev S. Vygotsky's *Thought and Language*. Bruner notes that Vygotsky has indeed "introduced an historical perspective into the understanding of how thought develops and, indeed, what thought is" (1962, ix). He goes on to say that it is to Vygotsky that Soviet psychologists turn in examining the manner in which "man fights free from the dominance of stimulus-response conditioning of the classic Pavlovian type" (x).

Indeed, we have cherished the contributions of the book *Thought and Language* since Vygotsky has shown us how to reason very tightly about word meanings and how these meanings lead us to begin our understanding of cognitive processes. He shows us that speech and speech patterns are social in their origins (1962). We now know that there is a fundamental understanding within speech communities that the words used and the concepts they represent almost always are purposeful and reflective of internalized verbal thought. To Vygotsky a word is a microcosm of human consciousness (1962). Moreover, within this remarkable book Vygotsky demonstrates the role of school instruction in the development of higher mental operations. It is important to recall the amazing insights that are offered in the following passage:

> The leading idea in the following discussion can be reduced to this formula: the relation of thought to word is not a thing but a process, a continual movement back and forth from thought to word and from word to thought. In that process, the relation of thought to word undergoes changes which themselves may be regarded as development in the functional sense. Thought is not merely expressed in words; it comes into existence through them. Every thought tends to connect something with something else, to establish a relationship between things. Every thought moves, grows and develops, fulfills a function, solves a problem. This flow of thought occurs as an inner movement through a series of planes. An analysis of the interaction of thought and word must begin with an investigation of the different phases and planes that thought traverses before it is embodied in words.
>
> The first thing such a study reveals is the need to distinguish between two planes of speech. Both the inner, meaningful, semantic aspect of speech and the external, phonetic aspect, though forming a true unity, have their own laws of movement. The unity of speech is a complex, not a homogenous, unity. (125)

Vygotsky offers us early theoretical proof through sound reasoning that there is, in fact, a different kind of process that goes on when we talk about word development as opposed to thought development. Simply stated, Vygotsky shows us that words are related to thoughts but do not necessarily shape them. Likewise, thoughts are made up of words but are not necessarily dependent upon them. Vygotsky points out that their difference is the first stage of a close union (126). He shows us that thought and word are not cut from one pattern. In a sense, there may be more differences than likenesses. He also demonstrates, citing Jean Piaget, that children use subordinate clauses with *because* and *although* and so forth long before they grasp the structures of meaning corresponding to these syntactic forms. Grammar precedes logic (127).

As we have seen previously, the linguistic parts of speech, namely morphology, phonology, syntax, and semantics, are inextricably linked yet maintain their own individual identity. What Vygotsky, Piaget, and Bruner help us to understand more clearly is that these kinds of linguistic notions elucidate not only the question of how we develop language and thought processes but also why we develop them.

This author, as a linguist, believes that Vygotsky's contribution is enormous while Piaget's is insightful. It is no surprise that the field of linguistics continues to grapple with the notion of the development of grammar and the development of phonology and speech patterns. We know clearly that children use language, but we do not know necessarily how we can intervene in the process of their developing language. Now since this chapter, indeed this book, is concerned with education reform, let us return to the notion of why semantics provides us with an explanation of the failure of education reform.

Noam Chomsky, the prolific and renowned linguist and social activist, recently published an interesting book called *Chomsky on Miseducation* (2000). Chomsky's work focuses not only on issues of language but also on specifically how politics, power, justice, and social change become essential to any chance of true education reform. Chomsky illuminates the discussion with these words:

> Education is, of course, in part a matter of schools and colleges and the formal information systems. That is true whether the goal of education is education for freedom and democracy, as Dewey advocated, or education for obedience and subordination and marginalization, as the dominant institutions require. The University of Chicago sociologist James Coleman, one of the main students of education and effects of experience on children's lives, concludes from many studies that the total effect of home background is considerably greater than the total effect of school variables in determining student achievement. So, it is therefore important to have a look at how social policy and the dominant culture are shaping these factors, home influences and so on. (48)

Chomsky's insights shed light on this chapter because of the implication that policymaking around education reform is deceptive in its simplification of a problem, namely the problem of children's lives and their achievement in school. We know from many studies and from our own experiential knowledge base that the results of school are not dependent solely upon what goes on in schools. Clearly, other factors prevail.

The semantics of education reform demand that we not only look at whether the words and the concepts are meaningful but whether the policies in which these words are used, in fact, change the actual quality of lives and the educational outcomes of schools. If we are to accept that school outcome is much broader than what goes on in schools, then we must accept that we have to look at other areas in order to measure the results of schooling (Apple, 1999). Standardized tests measure a lot more of the accidental knowledge that students have as opposed to the fundamental knowledge of the curriculum. (This idea will be explored fully in chapter 5.) However, we need now to consider the implications of the meanings that have taken hold and the implications for the continued failure of the educational enterprise.

RECONCEPTUALIZATION OF REFORM AND ITS MEANINGS

If we are to believe that the raison d'être of education reform resides in the indisputable fact of educational failure, then it behooves us to understand exactly what the reform policies actually mean. It is clear that the simple act of implementing education reform in the fifty states has not demonstrated a better model of educating the American child. We know this because we continue to strive for the perfect reform package. What is it that keeps us spending time, money, and energy on reforming a school system that has demonstrated a relative degree of success in terms of the numbers of students who can read, who graduate, and who in fact secure jobs within the economy of the United States? The answer to this question is beyond this author's area of expertise.

I am quite certain, however, that the answer lies at an intersecting point of a large number of disciplines such as economics, philosophy, sociology, political science, and psychology. Yet this is not the primary concern of this book. The concern of this chapter, indeed this book, is to discover some meaningful and fundamental principles upon which to carry out the improvement of the quality of the life of the children who spend an enormous amount of time in school. We already understand clearly that the school does not exist in isolation; it is a microcosm of society, and it interrelates continually with other segments of the economy and the daily operations of our country. Our concern then is to reconceptualize not only the policies but also the language that is embedded in these policies so that we can talk about the problem in ways that are more productive and more closely directed toward creating a better life for everyone. What would this take?

I happened to see a commentary on American schooling by the conservative educational theorist Jacques Barzun that aired on C-Span on January 7, 2002. In this program Barzun was speaking at Trinity University in San Antonio, Texas, on October 24, 2001. His comments were, I believe, insightful and useful for our discussion of the semantics of education reform and the concepts that are embedded in it. Professor Barzun said that we need to return to teaching *knowledge* or risk a return to barbarism. He further stated that the main function of school is to remove ignorance. I found that to be an interesting notion, the idea that the function of school is to remove a condition that we would believe a student came to us with, namely ignorance. While this idea leads falsely to a conclusion that the student is at the center of choice between success and failure in school, I found Professor Barzun's comments to actually have a great deal of insight. In fact, we all have witnessed an exponential rise in the amount of violence in schools within the past decade. We have all sensed that there is a fundamental problem that we can neither identify nor solve easily. It is precisely because of this sense that we have continued to allow the development of solutions which have been transposed into education reform proposals, acts, and legislation. We should know instinctively that these legislative acts are not matched to the real problem and cannot succeed. As Barzun put it, "There have been many proposals, schemes, studies, experiments since 1950, and none have led to reform or to improvements that anyone is satisfied with." (Barzun, 2001)

For Professor Barzun a major turning point in the demise of schools (that is, when schools turned away from their central mission of transmitting knowledge) was in 1918 when the Commission on the Reorganization of Secondary Education, a committee of the National Education Association, issued what would end up being one of the most significant educational reports of the past century. The title of the report, *The Cardinal Principles of Secondary Education,* calls upon secondary educators to broaden their goals and to prepare students for the challenges of life. As we have seen in chapter 3, *The Cardinal Principles* was a far-reaching document because it included seven broad areas of life: health; command of fundamental processes (basic academic skills); worthy home membership; vocation; civic education; worthy use of leisure; and ethical character. While these seven principles reflect the progressive movement in education espoused by John Dewey, they mark, at the same time, as Barzun points out, a significant change in the direction of curriculum development in the American school system. Barzun was obviously displeased with the fact that schools have become the harbinger of so many societal issues and he understood that the schools are unable to successfully deliver a liberal arts education never mind take on such a broad agenda. Yet today reform, it would seem, must address both schools and society—at the least. Or, as Bourdieu might reason: Since privilege and cultural capital can be seen to reproduce, unconsciously, the conditions of their own reproduction (1977), it becomes necessary to conceive of school reform in the broadest terms despite the positivist tendency to look for easy, sentential responses to complex issues.

CONCLUSION

In *The Sociology of Language,* Joshua Fishman gives an eloquent discussion of the social nature of language development and use (1972). He points out, for example:

> That there are more pervasive and therefore seemingly less systematic ways in which lexicons in particular and languages as a whole are reflective of the speech communities that employ them. In a very real sense, a language variety is an inventory of the concerns and interests of those who employ it at any given time. If any portion of this inventory reveals features not present in other portions, this may be indicative of particular stresses or influences in certain interaction networks within the speech community as a whole or in certain role relationships within the community's total role repertoire. (166)

While I must forego for reasons of space limitations a technical treatment of all the implications that it would seem Fishman intends in the above discourse, I nonetheless want to point out that it is very relevant to our discussion of the semantics of education reform. It should be clear that the language choices (words, concepts) of policymakers are, in large part, *intentional.* What this implies beyond the fact of purpose is that the policies themselves are an attempt to make the public at large believe that reform legislation, along with billions of dollars of expenditure, will help solve serious failures that are noted within the educational system. What Fishman contributes to our discussion is the fact that *the language choices of policymakers are lexical items understood by other policymakers but lacking in significant content for the educational practitioner who faces a different set of pressures in the classroom every day.* For example, the notion of "governance" that was discussed previously in this chapter (and in chapter 2) is a good example of where the word itself has been chosen to represent a problem, and thus the word itself has taken on a set of meanings particular to a group of policymakers who employs the word. The practitioners, meanwhile, understand that governance is simply this: the principal of the school who is in charge of the administrative tasks of that school and who does not understand governance to be a problem; nor does the practitioner understand governance to be in any way a critical issue to be addressed in order to improve schools and the achievement of students.

The now famous and classic Sapir-Whorfian hypothesis, which elucidates the question of influence of linguistic form on behavior as well as one's view of the world, demonstrates an interdependence between the use of language and the behavior one exhibits. Simply stated, the hypothesis demonstrates in convincing ways that the choice of language is limited by one's perception of the world. To apply this notion to our discussion of education reform, it becomes clear that policymakers view schools in a particular way and choose lexical items that are within their policies and within their language community. Their education reform acts reflect these views. Thus, governance, curriculum, and testing become the obsession of policymakers who really do not communicate in any sound linguistic way with the educational practitioners (that is, teachers) who face the overwhelming task of educating our country's children.

While it is very uncomfortable to ponder the importance of our discussion in this chapter, that is, the semantics of education reform as being a key issue, and one that implies neglect, I must nonetheless summarize this discussion of education reform as a pervasive set of educational atrocities. The checkered past of education reform throughout the fifty states points to a plutocratic tendency to address supposed educational failure by misusing language and making policy a tool for hegemonic practice under the guise of improving the educational outcomes of schooling. I must denounce all of these practices at the legislative level since my examination of reform legislation and acts has yielded these unmistakable truths about what has gone on for the past decade in the United States.

In the next chapter we will look at curriculum as knowledge and further explore how knowledge in the public domain becomes a different matter when we seek private significance. We will examine curriculum as a set of propositions, a set of knowledge, which schools attempt to transmit to students. While this is a very public act, we will see that its private significance has to do with the sum total of *all other experiences* that students have outside of schools and that constitute a more significant set of knowledge for each and every one of them.

PART II

CURRICULUM, INSTRUCTION, AND ASSESSMENT

Three Essentials Lost in Political and Hegemonic Maneuvering

CHAPTER 5

CURRICULUM AS KNOWLEDGE
Public vs. Private Significance

CURRICULUM IS AN ELUSIVE ENTITY in modern schooling, and nearly everyone has a strong opinion on what should constitute a school's curriculum. Yet it has become increasingly clear that changes in curriculum as part of the education reform movement have taken on a distinctly political tone. Both in rhetoric and substance the whole curriculum frameworks/guidelines effort, typically originated at the state level, has proceeded as if the addition, deletion, or modification of knowledge were neutral, value-free, and non-controversial. Nothing could be further from the truth.

This chapter will explore curriculum as knowledge that has very strong connections to culture and identity of citizens within a community. Moreover, both the public and private aspects of knowledge will be examined in light of current efforts in many states to homogenize curriculum and create tests to measure the extent to which students "know" information deemed important for effective participation in today's world.

The ASCD (Association for Supervision and Curriculum Development) in its 1985 yearbook, entitled *Current Thought on Curriculum* and edited by Alex Molnar, attempted to move away from a portrayal of the differences between the theoretical and practical worlds of curriculum development and instead to focus on the essential need for mutual cooperation between theoretician and practitioner. The ASCD in this yearbook bemoaned the fact that the academician and the teacher lived in substantially different worlds. Some of the main points that are relevant to this chapter will be outlined below.

SCHOOLS AND THEIR CURRICULUM: A CONTINUING CONTROVERSY

In *Current Thought on Curriculum* Molnar comments on what makes curriculum the vexing and controversial issue it continues to be. He traces the history of education and highlights the struggle it has had with political and social forces throughout history. Because of the historically unprecedented relationship between education and social forces, it is not surprising that Molnar would highlight as critical the need for schools to become comfortable with their role of incorporating social questions into the curriculum.

While it is well known that there have been numerous attempts to define curriculum in ways that allow for broad curriculum objectives to be met, it is also well known that these kinds of efforts have been based in behavioral types of models and have limited the kinds of questions that the curriculum is allowed to ask. For example, in Don Weinstein's book *Curriculum Mapping for Administrators* (1987), he points out that the more specific the questioning is the more likely it is that we are able to develop specific evaluation designs and determinations about outcomes and program costs. He points out that mapping may allow us to answer questions such as to what extent did the program deliver what it intended, to what extent are the texts and instructional materials and software appropriate, and to what extent are the tests that are used to measure success of the program useful and effective. While all of this sounds fairly simple and harmless, there is nonetheless a *pervasive exclusionary motif* that guides this kind of educational program. Although it is clear enough that one might develop tests to measure whether students learned discrete level knowledge, it is entirely another question to ask whether the choice of knowledge that is taught is, in fact, useful and appropriate in the first place. This issue will be explored in more depth later in this chapter.

Returning to the idea of the chapter itself, the question of the public versus the private significance of curriculum as knowledge is one that is most frequently ignored or marginalized. However, not to recognize as essential curriculum as a dynamic entity (knowledge) that is shaped and defined through cultural interaction, individual growth, and communal discourse is to miss the essential meaning of curriculum itself. When we begin to try to discuss the public significance of curriculum, we must begin to understand that curriculum development itself is a public activity in most cases. When curriculum is developed in order to be a guideline for teachers, it begins to take on a structure and a design that allow it to be taught and allows it to be tested. Even though, in most cases, curriculum development has an overall philosophy behind it, this philosophy is quickly translated into specific objectives, learning activities, and test items to measure the extent to which students have acquired knowledge. Again, the public nature of curriculum leaves us to question the motivations behind curriculum development activities that most frequently occur for the purpose of developing materials to be used in schools.

Let us now take a look at a typical design of curriculum development that might play itself out in a public domain. The very first activity that one might encounter is the development of a philosophy. Although it is difficult to characterize and generalize the philosophy of all curriculum that is taught in all schools in the United States, this author, through intense research and observation, has seen a repetitive pattern that holds up in most places when curriculum development is attempted. The design goes something like this:

1. *Philosophy*
The curriculum is usually a set of planned learning experiences organized for individual students to enable them to attain the educational goals established by a school system. Typically, the planned learning experiences, if done well, take into account things such as learning theory, instructional design, available strategies for teaching, the characteristics and needs of the learning, community values, parental expectations, teacher interest and expertise, and the specific goals of the community and school district.

2. *Rationale*
Curriculum development usually has a philosophy that takes on specific meaning within the local context of its development. What this means is that a rationale emerges based on the needs of the community to define a set of learning experiences in various subject matters for all students in the district.

3. *Content Delineation*
Since it is impossible to teach the entire knowledge base of any subject, it is necessary, usually, to delineate a specific sequence of content to be taught so that students receive instruction that is comprehensible and meaningful.

4. *Themes and Topics*

While it may not be explicitly stated, a scope and sequence of some kind and time allotments in most instances will be found within the curriculum development project. This is because the nature of knowledge in its pure form is not as teachable as knowledge that is attuned to the developmental age of the learner, that is, a series of topics are taught that are comprehensible to the student at a specific age and in a specific grade level.

5. *Texts and Materials*

It is usually understood that the teacher is not the holder of all the knowledge and that the public domain of knowledge allows us to select commercially produced textbooks and materials to distribute to students to assist them in meeting the educational objectives of the school system. In this day of high technology, this area of concern goes well beyond the historical audiovisual considerations. Computer hardware and software are accounted for and are incorporated into the curriculum development project.

6. *Methodologies/Strategies*

Be it research based on evidence or unproven, most development projects, at least peripherally, consider the issue of method. While it is well known in the daily life of teachers in schools that the method of choice is usually existential (that is, no method at all), it is nonetheless a part of curriculum development to consider which strategies will work better for certain groups of students. We know that it is unlikely that the predetermination of strategy in any learning environment is probably ill fated; it is nonetheless carried out in this way in most development projects. What the ASCD yearbook (1985) attempts to elucidate is the necessity to blend the two worlds, that is, the world of theory with the world of practice. When this is done well, the selection of strategy can reflect an existential philosophy and respond immediately within the learning experience of the classroom to whatever students appear to need in order to learn at that moment.

7. *Implementation*

The question of implementation sounds parochial, yet it is nonetheless an important phase of curriculum development to know when and how a new curriculum or a new set of materials will be implemented and among which student population. The consideration of implementing a set of curriculum guidelines or new objectives is an important phase of the entire curriculum development process. Deciding when and how to implement is as necessary as deciding when to test and when to begin a new lesson with a group of students.

8. *Assessment*
While the topic of assessment will be taken up in chapter 7, suffice it to say now that within a curriculum development activity that is essentially public there is little room beyond standardization of results for truly assessing the extent to which students learn what we teach them. What I mean is that it is unlikely that there will be considerable effort put in along the lines of portfolios or other authentic assessments since the public at large, while well intentioned and interested in the individual growth of each and every student, is nonetheless more interested in a summary of educational outcome preferably delivered in numeric form. Standardized testing is indeed alive and well and it is projected that it will attain a ripe old age if not become immortal.

9. *Program Evaluation*
While most program evaluations are formative in that they assume the continued existence of the program, there should be and sometimes must be designs that include summative approaches. Summative approaches allow for the discontinuation of programs that simply do not work. While there are lots of threats in today's political climate to close schools that do not meet objectives and that fail large numbers of students, it is nonetheless more common to seek a formative approach to each and every school regardless of success rate of that school.

Let us now return to our consideration of curriculum as knowledge and take a close look at the private significance of this endeavor. Having outlined a typical curriculum development process that inevitably leads to a set of learning experiences for students, it is nonetheless inescapable that knowledge does not easily issue from the public process just outlined. Students are individualistic and are resistant to overly systematized educational environments.

The private nature of acquiring knowledge requires attention to several areas informed by psychology: motivation, intellectual stimulation, language acquisition, critical thinking, creative thinking, personal well-being, and interpersonal skill. Since it is well known that psychology has informed curriculum development for at least the past fifty years, it is convenient to begin a discussion of the private nature of knowledge by taking a look at the aspects just listed within the field of psychology.

First, let us discuss motivation and intellectual stimulation. Recognizing that learning is a lifelong process, we must seek in all cases to instill in students a desire to acquire knowledge that may be utilized to address present and future problems. The difficulty in instilling this kind of desire is that students will not necessarily be motivated to *complete our agenda* and might have the need to satisfy their own intellectual curiosity. What I mean is, if a student is not intellectually stimulated, the level of motivation that he or she has for learning what it is that the teacher is teaching will be low. Furthermore, it is more difficult to have students take responsibility for their own learning when motivation levels are not optimal. While reward and punishment work marginally and minimally, they are not a good long-term approach to achieving the educational objectives of schools. Motivation can be looked at as a flow of energy from within, and unless the flow of energy is triggered, there will be substantial and sufficient reason not to learn what it is that a student is being taught.

The second psychological aspect, language acquisition, is an increasingly important one in a diverse world where many speakers are not primarily proficient in English. In the United States the area of bilingual education, controversial as it is, takes on political tones that further complicates the discussion of language acquisition as a psychological aspect. While the majority of students in the United States at this time are primary speakers of English, it is well known that there is an increasing number of speakers of Spanish and Asian dialects that presents an interesting and complex array of problems to be solved. Indeed, by the year 2050, it is estimated that 30% of the public school-age population will be Hispanic, while 9% will be Asian (Newman, 2002, 275). Meanwhile, California, with its passage of Proposition 227 sponsored by Ronald Unz, has dealt with the issue of its large Hispanic population by mandating English as the primary language of instruction. Arizona has followed suit and has passed similar legislation, and Massachusetts was the most recent target of the Ronald Unz campaign to make English the only language of instruction within schools. While these political actions do not in any way enhance the educational process, they nonetheless make it inescapable for academics and educators to deal with these questions of language acquisition in ways that are political as well as psychological. Language acquisition in itself is a pure enterprise; it is one that is individualistic, and it is one that is complex in terms of knowledge acquisition. When students cannot understand instruction clearly, the amount of language acquisition goes down. Sustained intellectual development, especially development of linguistic skill, requires possession of proficient reading skills, well-developed writing skills, comprehensible speaking skills, and the ability to listen and comprehend the world around the learner. All of these are required in order to have an educational system that fosters individual growth of students.

Curriculum as Knowledge

The third psychological aspect, critical thinking, is a popular and somewhat trendy area of consideration. To think critically requires the ability to analyze, and the kinds of questions posed to students within the classroom will usually either foster a critical thinking process or deter this process from occurring at all.

The fourth aspect is personal well-being. Without the attributes of physical and emotional health, it is difficult to progress toward other educational goals. To cope with the stresses and strains of life in the twenty-first century, students will need to come to grips with many public concerns in a very personal way. Every effort should be made to help students develop confidence and self-esteem and to organize a set of personal goals and aspirations so that the complex array of issues in the public domain do not overwhelm the efforts of personal growth in the private domain. Schools have the responsibility to provide a framework within which students may learn to exercise sound judgment and define and abide by individual and community values as well as conduct themselves in line with moral and ethical standards.

The last psychological aspect to consider is interpersonal skill. While schools have the obligation to teach students to work constructively with others in groups and teach them to understand the world around them, they have a greater responsibility to make students aware of the interconnectedness of society with human activity and the environment and, moreover, to understand the interdependence of these disparate worlds. Students need to develop cooperation skills and conflict resolution skills in order to be able to function well on an interpersonal level. In order to practice and hone these skills as well as other social skills such as communication, respect, trust, consideration, and caring, schools need to broadly educate students in ways that foster intense personal growth.

Now that we have looked at the fundamental differences between knowledge in the public domain and the knowledge in the private domain (or rather, knowledge acquisition in these two domains), let us consider the kinds of knowledge that are likely to occur within a classroom setting. It is important to note that this discussion is one that is never found within the reform literature or within any reform acts that this author has studied, which includes a review of all education reform efforts in all fifty states of the United States.

The two kinds of knowledge that will be discussed here are fundamental knowledge and accidental knowledge. It is interesting that either or both kinds of knowledge can lead to essential knowledge acquisition and give rise to elaborated features of the objects, ideas, and issues in the world around us. *Fundamental knowledge* includes the areas of study within the curriculum that are generally termed "core" or "basic skills" and generally refers to a relatively agreed upon set of "facts" that most teachers would agree to include in a curriculum within a school. This definition of fundamental knowledge is in no way intended to be comprehensive since this author is well aware of the arguments surrounding cultural phenomena that impact the determination of a basic set of skills or a basic set of knowledge. Nonetheless, it is important that we draw a distinction between the knowledge that is taught in schools, which is fundamental, and the second kind of knowledge—accidental—which tends to be acquired outside of formal settings. As previously noted, either kind of knowledge can lead to essence or elaboration, but each kind leads to them in distinctly different ways.

To continue, let us consider accidental knowledge. *Accidental knowledge* is the kind of knowledge that is acquired as one goes about one's life. It is not necessarily knowledge acquired about history or mathematics or any other formalized field of study, but, rather, it is the kind of knowledge that one acquires experientially. For example, when dealing with people, knowing whether one is dealing with a person of good character or bad character is, in these days, accidental knowledge. Why? Schools have long ago abandoned, in general, any moral or character education that was a feature of the educational system in the United States up until perhaps the late 1960s or early 1970s. The abandonment of this kind of education, that is, character education, has relegated the acquisition of this kind of important life skill, namely, knowing the type of person with whom one is dealing, to the realm of accidental knowledge. Now it is well known that through experience and/or intuition we would be able to acquire a general idea about the kind of person with whom we are dealing; however, since it is no longer part of the formal curriculum, it is now part of accidental knowledge. Therefore, a potentially dangerous situation exists because, by definition, it is not taught within the formal school curriculum and, therefore, whether one acquires this kind of knowledge is left to chance.

The achievement of essence, or rather the understanding of essence, and the acquisition of an elaborated set of features about any idea or object can be considered by-products of both the formal education system, that is, fundamental knowledge, and the experiential system of learning, that is, accidental knowledge. Both essence and elaboration tend to be elusive within the formal structure of schooling. The best argument for this and the best evidence that this is true exists in the announced and mandated outcomes of education reform. As mentioned previously in chapters 1 and 2, the results of reform methods have been dismal in most states, and there has not been, in any state, a substantial and significant increase in achievement. Now it has already been pointed out by this author that the goal of increasing achievement, in and of itself, is not necessarily a well thought out plan to improve schooling since achievement levels can only be measured if we are *certain* that we know the baseline achievement level of the students whose acquisition of knowledge we are measuring.

Another important issue that surfaces when we talk about the acquisition of knowledge is, as Tobin Hart (2001) points out, "Besides the elevation of knowledge to the status of Truth, contemporary education tends to teach as if the 'objective' scientific fact provides the only valid source of information and knowledge" (58). Hart's treatment of the patterns of knowledge lends support to the idea that schools favor "objective" knowledge over "unobjective" knowledge, for lack of a better term. Hart further elaborates and points to a "tyranny of truth" (58), and he offers an alternative that he defines as four distinct kinds of knowledge, each with its own validity claims or requirements for truth. He draws from Ken Wilbur's (1995) synthesis. Let me note that Hart's identification of four kinds of knowledge is not in direct conflict with this author's previous delineation of fundamental and accidental knowledge as the two categories of knowledge. Instead, they tend to complement each other, and Hart's treatment with Wilbur's synthesis provides further explanation of the problem of knowledge acquisition.

The first of the four distinct kinds of knowledge that Hart identifies is called exterior-individual. He says that exterior-individual knowledge is of the empirical and behavioral type and that "it is an explanation of what is 'out there,'" including the construction of a taxonomy of plants or the investigation of seretonin levels in the brain. This is, of course, knowledge that is gathered through observation and can be measured. The second kind of knowledge that Hart identifies is called exterior-social. The difference between this kind of knowledge and the exterior-individual kind is simply that the former considers "interacting systems instead of focusing primarily on individuals" (59). In other words, this kind of knowledge resides in the realm of systems theory and is more holistic in its approach.

The third kind of knowledge that Hart has identified is called interior-individual. Unlike exterior knowledge, interior knowledge originates from within the individual and has its source in one's own ways of identifying what is important in the world. As Hart explains, "When we look at a piece of art or a beautiful sunset, feel deep compassion or moral outrage, have a moment of revelation and insight, we experience some quality of meaning and value within us that we can not adequately reduce to a measurable quantity" (60).

The fourth and last kind of knowledge is called interior-cultural. Much like the first kind of interior-generated knowledge, this kind, of course, is the conglomeration or the accumulation of what one perceives subjectively about the world. It is the kind of knowledge that is generated over time and tends to cluster in meaningful ways based on one's own distinct ways of organizing the world. What is distinctly different about these four kinds of knowledge and the knowledge that is typically imparted through classroom instruction in schools is that the four kinds that Hart has identified are multidimensional and avoid the positivists' tradition that invariably leads to a one-dimensional view of knowledge and, indeed, of the world.

To go beyond what Hart has so eloquently attempted to identify in terms of knowledge structures and knowledge acquisition, this author would like to expand upon Hart's thinking and return to the category that identifies fundamental versus accidental knowledge. Hart's four types of knowledge are really best categorized as accidental. And it is no small irony that what Hart identifies is the kind of knowledge that most of us value in our daily lives. This brings up the question, Why is the fundamental knowledge category so important at all? Then this, asked another way, brings up the question of why have formal schooling at all? This is a very complex issue and one that this author will attempt to clarify in the next section.

FUNDAMENTAL KNOWLEDGE: ESSENCE AND ELABORATION

In order to shed some light on the nature of fundamental knowledge, it is useful to go back to the arguments made in this chapter concerning curriculum development. We noted that curriculum development, as a process, tends to be discrete and tends to lead the whole educational process toward identification of knowledge that can be measured. Now when we talk about fundamental knowledge, we are now faced with the contrast of school knowledge as opposed to all knowledge that is acquired outside of school. Both kinds of knowledge (fundamental and accidental) have the possibility of being *essential* or *elaborated*. Essential knowledge in schools tends to proceed from the curriculum development process. Furthermore, curriculum development, in and of itself, is carried out typically for one of four purposes (Glatthorn, 1995). The four purposes of curriculum development work are: restructuring, development, renewal, and enablement. Restructuring is the preferred approach to the curriculum work when the school, as an organization, wishes to create brand-new learning experiences for its students. Typically, restructuring begins with outcomes and then designs learning experiences to meet the desired outcomes (Spady, 1988).

The second purpose for carrying out curriculum work is development. Development is similar to restructuring, but it is a phase that attempts to further identify the particulars of the learning experiences in which one wishes to have students engage. The third purpose, renewal, tends to be an activity

Curriculum as Knowledge

of fine tuning *existing* curricula. And the fourth and last purpose is enablement, which is the process that is used to move a curriculum plan to the actual delivery phase of schooling, that is, the question of how to encourage teachers to actually use the new curriculum product.

All of the above curriculum work and its four purposes tend to clarify the essence of fundamental knowledge. As far as elaborated knowledge, the primary concern and ultimate determination of whether elaboration takes place has to do with a long-standing debate in the research literature over breadth versus depth of curriculum. While there is no absolute conclusion to this debate, recent research tends to confirm that depth matters more than simple coverage (Glatthorn, 1995). It is something more than pure common sense to reach this conclusion; however, it is not beyond the realm of pure reason to conclude that breadth of knowledge is less and less possible as information explodes through the use of the Internet. Or, perhaps, easy access to the Internet will empower even more the advocates of "depth."

Because curriculum development is a political process (Giroux, 1980; Apple and Beyer, 1998), it is easy to understand how power plays a key role as the curriculum development process proceeds. In everyday terms, turf is fought over and the whole development process becomes problematic in that certain questions are allowed and others are not. Furthermore, as knowledge is *elaborated,* there is a danger that the fundamental knowledge being taught in schools becomes grangerized (that is, pieced together in encyclopedia fashion) and incoherent. It is, of course, a very undesirable outcome of curriculum development and of schooling in general that fundamental knowledge takes on the aura of incoherence. However, it is posited that one of the main problems of the whole educational enterprise is that instruction by teachers is not understood by students (author's observations over thirty years). It is this author's position that the failure of education reform in general has more to do with the miscommunication and misunderstanding at the delivery stage of curriculum (that is, when teachers attempt to implement the product of curriculum development).

> Part of what education lacks is imagination.
> When we build closed systems of knowledge, imagination is irrelevant,
> even a disturbance, and so it typically receives only token attention, if at all.
> (Hart, 2001, 68)

It is clear that fundamental knowledge, the preoccupation of schooling, cannot and will not ever encourage students to engage in imagination and exploration of what it is to know something in depth. While it is true that schools give the appearance of trying to elaborate the fundamental knowledge that it imparts to students (through project work, and so forth), it will never be able to approach the kind of richness that accidental knowledge provides. We have seen in this chapter that knowledge as a result of accident is more integral than knowledge acquired in schools. Michael Apple (1990) makes the point very well that schools have all along intended to provide discrete level knowledge that serves the larger social order. He observes quite well the fact that the meanings that are transmitted in schools are, in fact, precisely the meanings that reinforce an orderly society with its social stratification and economic inequities intact. Other researchers have concluded similarly on this matter (Giroux and Aronowitz, 1985; Bowles and Gintis, 1976; Freire 2000).

To ignore the ways of knowing that cognitive science has contributed to our own understanding of curriculum is to risk a repetition of teaching in a fundamentalist tradition that continues to focus exclusively on "knowing that and knowing how" at the expense of "knowing if." Hart, citing Gray (1968), points out that Greek philosophers distinguished between "the fact that" and "the reason why" (Hart, 2001). This distinction itself, while useful, does not even go far enough in terms of showing the limitations of fundamental knowledge. Indeed, fundamental knowledge can involve both factual information and explanations as to why certain facts relate to others. *However*, it is the philosophical knowing "if" knowledge is worth acquiring at all that separates fundamental knowledge from accidental knowledge. The reason that this is true is as follows: With accidental knowledge, one always gets to choose whether one cares to learn a specific set of facts or skills, and so forth. In school, however, students do not have a choice as to what they should or should not care to learn. They must learn the curriculum as it has been developed and as it is taught. The obvious limitations of this should be apparent to even the most unindoctrinated reader of curriculum theory. Clearly, schools, if they engage in fundamental knowledge at the exclusion of a richer array of learning experiences, then schools are missing a very important part of the entire growth and development of its students. As Hart (2001) points out, citing Gardner (1991), neither teachers nor students are willing to undertake "risks for understanding"; instead, they content themselves with safer "correct answer compromises" and similar strategy. Under such compromises, education is considered a success if students are able to provide answers that have been sanctioned as correct (150). And Hart in the same work offers this gem: "The way we know affects both what we know and ultimately who we are, our state of being and well-being. Our style of knowing may invite us to meet the world as a problem to be solved, as beauty to behold, or as a concept to categorize" (65).

CONCLUSION

As John Miller points out, "A soulful curriculum recognizes and gives priority to the inner life. It seeks a balance and connection between our inner and outer lives. Traditionally, schools have ignored the child's inner life; in fact, our whole culture tends to ignore the inner life. The child's and adolescent's lives are filled with TV, videos, computer games, with little unstructured time" (Miller, 2000, 49).

The whole idea of the philosophical "knowing if" is clearly connected to the inner self. Educators know very well that having students memorize facts is not the kind of high-level, intelligent thinking that we want students to exercise within schools. Nonetheless, it is obvious, and has been pointed out previously, that the educational system produces exactly what it intends through its curriculum development process. Education reform aside, curriculum development as an activity never infuses a curriculum of "knowing if" and consistently produces students who can function well at the "know that" and "know how" levels. Why is this not enough?

The public and private significance of curriculum as knowledge requires that we force a new thinking within schooling so that the learning experience within schools can begin to transcend its own historical asphyxia. Yet we know very well and have known for quite a long time that the sources of the curriculum of schools are not linear and are not obvious to the bare eye. The sources of the curriculum are, for better or worse, a direct line to the larger social order that schools seek to maintain. Everyone understands what the planned curriculum means; everyone understands what the taught and the learned curricula are (Glatthorn, 1991).

This author wants to focus attention on an additional source of curriculum that is sometimes not included in discussion within curriculum theory. I am referring to what I call "the ignored curriculum." What this is in my view is the null curriculum, that is, the facts and skills that are never tested and that begin to reflect in explicit and implicit ways the accidental curriculum that students invariably *bring with them* to school since the accidental knowledge of a person is, by definition, part of the inner self. The reason that I highlight this ignored curriculum is precisely because it consists of all the rich and varied experiences that a person has engaged in and that end up making the person what he or she is. The difficulty with this idea is how it fits into the ongoing educational research and theory of which there is exceptional abundance. I believe that the ignored curriculum consists of all the unintended "learnings" with which the school is unable and unwilling to cope. Large class sizes, discipline problems, and too few resources all combine along with many other factors to make it impossible for teachers to "deal with" the inner self of the child. And, I believe, this failing to deal with the accidental knowledge, which is, by definition, part of one's private domain, has more significance in the long run for what kind of society we create than does the fundamental knowledge that is embodied in the curriculum as we now know it.

In chapter 4 we have seen the issue of coherence within the educational system. I discussed the implications for the misuse of words and concepts, or rather the use of words and concepts devoid of meaning, and pointed out how education reform, in and of itself, has done nothing to address (or perhaps has created) this very serious endemic problem within the whole educational enterprise. The question of coherence is a key one for the following reason: If students do not understand what the words and concepts mean (much in the same way that teachers assign different meanings to the ideas and concepts of policymakers as we saw in chapter 4), they of course will not acquire the skills that the system wanted them to acquire. It is no surprise then that the results of the educational system are abysmally low and continue to be low even with intense education reform efforts across the country. If coherence is agreed upon as a critical part of a sound and effective educational system, then there is no surprise that the current educational system is failing miserably. Students' need for a coherent set of ideas is lacking precisely because the education reform efforts have been fragmented. How do we remedy this?

In the third part of this book, I will offer suggestions on how to move toward solutions to this persistent problem. I will call upon "reinventing" the system, keeping radical and proven methodology and incorporating the best of thinking from all disciplines that inform, and benefit from, educational theory and research.

CHAPTER 6

INSTRUCTION AS THEORY
The Wide Gap between Talking and Walking

AS WE HAVE SEEN IN PREVIOUS CHAPTERS, education reform legislation has had a series of obstacles in terms of its achieving outcomes commensurate with the amount of time, energy, and expenditure of money and resources that the reform legislations across the fifty states have required. Radical changes in the ways that teachers deliver curriculum have not proven in any way to be a result of the legislation across the fifty states for several reasons. One of the major reasons involves the fact that reform legislation rarely takes up the issue of teaching methodology. Yet a more significant reason is the fact that radical changes in instructional methodology seem to elude any comprehensive approach to reshaping teaching and learning so that achievement levels will show gains that are in line with the kind of massive reforms envisioned in the legislation. Indeed, one can only find minor changes in teaching technique if one examines the general delivery of instruction across schools in the United States. What has been needed and continues to be needed is a fundamental change in the way that schools are organized for learning, and we have yet to begin to fulfill this kind of a promise.

In this chapter we will examine how instruction as a science and as a theoretical and empirical object of study has not made its way into American classrooms nearly to the extent that one would have expected based on the amount of information available and based on the great desire on the part of almost everyone for schools to respond to societal changes. Not only is instruction not varied enough, but it is also not based on the extensive research findings that have remained largely ignored and very infrequently used. It will be demonstrated that the number and depth of instructional methodologies available in the literature have indeed not in any way made their way to fruition in actual classroom settings.

MORE THAN A HALF CENTURY OF THEORETICAL WORK

Numerous theorists over the past half century have demonstrated that instruction as a science is a reasonable object of study for cognitive psychologists and others who want to demonstrate how to approach the delivery of curriculum in schools. Jerome Bruner in one of his classic works (1966) explores the question of how cognitive growth and development occur, and he offers four principles for a theory of instruction: (1) it should specify how to predispose the learner; (2) it should specify the structure of the knowledge; (3) it should identify the sequencing of the knowledge; and (4) it should specify the nature of the pacing and rewards.

Bruner went on to demonstrate (for example, using the social studies curriculum M:ACOS [Man: A Course of Study] as a model) that a teacher could guide learning in the natural way and that it should be guided without undue pressure on the learner. Learning, therefore, creates a situation in which natural curiosity can be fostered almost as an involuntary act. Of course, Bruner had previously developed a context for the above four principles in his work, *The Process of Education*. He notes:

> Our cultural climate has not been marked traditionally by a deep appreciation of intellectual values. We have as a people always expressed a great faith in education. There are many reasons for this—the absence of an aristocracy, the pragmatic demands inherent in a frontier society, and so on. (1960, 73)

And Bruner admits, at the time (in the 1960s), that "Many Americans have become conscious, not just of the practical virtues of education, but of its content in quality—what it is and what it might be" (74). Further analysis of Bruner's work (1960, 1966) reveals a preoccupation with motivation on the part of the learner and seems to put the onus on the student in terms of outcome. Now it should not be interpreted here that Bruner focused all of his attention on the learner, but rather he acknowledged that a key piece of the puzzle of educational outcome involves the initial response of the learner, that is, the student's motivation to learn. Furthermore, in his work on instruction (1966), his program for evolving a theory of instruction, in addition to the above four principles, included a full and comprehensive analysis of the entire process of education. It should be noted that Bruner's work reemphasized that of Ralph Tyler (1949), and others, who offered paradigms to guide the development of curriculum and instructional theory. More specifically, the components of learner motivation, content of the curriculum, ordering and sequencing knowledge, and delivery of instruction all have been addressed by many theorists, not the least of whom include such icons as Tyler and Bruner.

Any attempt to illustrate the foundational work on instructional theory would be neglectful if it did not include a mention, however brief, of the educational theorist John Dewey. As early as 1900, and continuing until 1938, Dewey published several works that addressed the issue of the school and its necessity to focus on a child-centered curriculum and instructional program. Dewey especially noted (*The Child and the Curriculum*, 1902) that children need experiences in the classroom that will guide them toward an understanding of their environment. He noted that the child-centered school is one where methods should not be distinctly different for separate subjects but rather that the overall experience should be wholistic and balanced. Dewey believed in placing knowledge in the hands of children so that they might be able to create and re-create meaningful interpretations of the world around them (1902, 1916, 1938). While Dewey was not specifically concerned with creating a theory of instruction, his work nonetheless set the stage for the more focused attempts to define a theory of instruction and to articulate specific methodologies for use by teachers in actual classrooms.

No shortage exists in terms of the number of educational theorists who would continue, beyond the mid-1960s, to attempt to develop a theory of instruction. Gagne (1967); Gardner (1983, 1991); Adler (1982); Eisner (1985); Elkind (1978, 1993); Freire (1972), and many others all have contributed enormously to our understanding of what constitutes good teaching. Nonetheless, one author stands out in his consolidated and in-depth presentation of the field of instructional theory as one who has contributed the most to our understanding of what constitutes a good instructional program. I am referring to Bruce Joyce, who, along with the coauthor Marsha Weil (1972), identified more than twenty models of teaching that, when taken together, constitute the most elaborate and rich source of information about instruction that is, and has been, available for more than thirty years. *Models of Teaching* (1996) is an amazing compilation of theoretical models for use in classrooms. (I will return to an analysis of this rich resource but only after a consideration of a practitioner who, by virtue of his ability to apply instructional theory, has claimed an enormous share of the educational market in terms of guiding teachers to improve their instruction.)

Let us now take a look at this practitioner: Jon Saphier, who, along with Robert Gower (1979), offered so-called parameters within which instructional exchanges evolve and revolve. Saphier and Gower were indeed aware of most, if not all, of the instructional theorists identified in this chapter and drew upon the same studies that Joyce and Weil utilize in their compilation *Models of Teaching*. Thus there is reciprocity in terms of the material drawn upon, but there is a difference in the purpose for utilizing the material: Joyce and Weil compile the best of empirical data from the knowledge base on instruction while Saphier and Gower *utilize* the research base to improve the actual delivery of curriculum within schools. The latter develop a repertoire of useful teaching ideas in order to build teaching skills among educators in professional development settings. Indeed, Saphier's work has been widely published and disseminated among teachers, not only in the Northeast but throughout the United States and even internationally.

Let us now consider fifteen parameters of *The Skillful Teacher:*

1. *Attention*
This parameter addresses the question of whether students are attending to tasks and are engaged in the curriculum activity consistently over a class lesson or period of time. It also addresses the question of whether the teacher has an appropriate range of attention moves and whether those moves are working.

2. *Momentum*
This addresses the question of whether students are free from interruption, waiting time, distractions, and delay. It also speaks to a teacher's ability to keep the flow of events moving with smooth, rapid transition.

3. *Expectations*
Do students know exactly what is expected of them? Are the standards appropriate? Does the teacher communicate clearly? Are the standards high, yet attainable? Is the message sent that all students can learn?

4. *Personal Relationship Building*
The issue here is whether students show respect and regard for the teacher. Also, it is important that a teacher build good relationships with students.

5. *Discipline*
Are particularly resistant students dealt with appropriately? Does the teacher have a repertoire for working with resistant students?

6. *Principles of Learning*
This addresses the question of whether students' experiences show opportune use of the principles of learning. Also in question is the teacher's ability to build productive uses of principles of learning.

7. *Clarity*
Do all students understand the information and procedures? Is the teacher a good explainer? Does the teacher present accurate information?

8. *Space*
Does the room arrangement support instruction? Does the teacher get the most out of the arrangement of space and furniture?

9. *Time*
The issue in this parameter deals with the amount of time students are afforded to learn. Also in question here is the pace of the lesson, the beginning and ending of the lesson in terms of appropriate use of time, and a teacher's planning and management skills so that instructional time is used productively.

10. *Routines*
Do students follow efficient routines for all regularly recurring business within the classroom?

11. *Models of Teaching*
Are the students experiencing an identifiable model of teaching? Is it appropriate? Can the teacher match different students and learning goals with different models of teaching?

12. *Objectives*
Is there a clear, appropriate objective embedded in the instruction? Has the teacher decided upon a clear objective and framed it properly? Are objectives at the correct level of difficulty?

13. *Evaluation*
Do students receive systematic evaluation of their performance? Does the teacher know what the students have really learned?

14. *Learning Experiences*
In this parameter the issue is whether learning experiences in the classroom are appropriate for students, considering variables such as cognitive level, amount of structure, competition, cooperation, resources used, grouping, as well as other relevant variables. Also in question is whether the teacher is able to adjust learning experiences according to the needs and learning styles of the students.

15. *Organization of Curriculum*
Does the teacher plan learning experiences so that they show continuity, sequence, and integration with other learning experiences?

MODELS OF TEACHING
COMPILED BY BRUCE JOYCE AND MARSHA WEIL

As previously noted, Joyce and Weil (1996) offer more than twenty models in their excellent compilation of instructional theory, a book that is now classic and has been available to educators since 1972. While the work of Joyce and Weil was not intended to reflect, or be synchronized with, that of Saphier and Gower, it is nonetheless interesting to note that both pairs of researchers/theorists endeavored to explore the field of instruction during approximately the same time period, that is, since the 1970s.

As already pointed out, the work of Saphier and Gower was an immediate attempt to apply the instructional theories as they were developing or as they were in their infancy of development, whereas Joyce and Weil attempted to compile the best thinking in the field of instructional theory available as of 1972. In its five editions since 1972, *Models of Teaching* has included additions and elaborations of the models.

I will now explain the impact of *Models of Teaching* on the field of education and illustrate that its focus on brain processes has been the major focus of the vast majority of models explained by the authors. Indeed, if "Learning is a consequence of thinking" (1992, 8), then David Perkins has summarized eloquently the major importance of the work by Joyce and Weil that has contributed greatly to our appreciation and understanding of how thinking processes function within the educational setting.

As previously mentioned, there are more than twenty models available and it is the premise of this chapter that very few of the models have made their way to the implementation stage in actual classrooms. This is not in any way an indictment of teachers who struggle every day to educate their students. Rather, it is a sad commentary on the state of educational research and its ability to find its way into the arena of improving educational outcomes. The authors claim that there are nine models that are most commonly used and applicable to teaching (399). They are

1. Advance organizer;
2. Cooperative learning;
3. Jurisprudential model;
4. Synectics;
5. Concept attainment;
6. Inquiry training;
7. Assists to memory;
8. Role playing;
9. Inductive thinking.

It is the experience of this author in teaching a graduate curriculum theory and evaluation course over nine years (between 1984 and 1993) that of the nine models just listed there are no more than three that are frequently used and can be observed during a "typical" lesson in a school in Massachusetts. The research base for this particular conclusion involves more than 650 students who enrolled in this author's course and who were assigned the task of identifying two or three of the nine models that were common or frequently utilized in instruction in their particular school or their particular school system. No more than three models were found to be represented in the various school districts in which the 650 educators worked. In fact, the vast majority of graduate students reported that the most commonly implemented (admittedly by chance that is, the teacher implementing the model was not aware that he or she was implementing a defined model) were: advance organizer, cooperative learning, and concept attainment. For a detailed description of the aforementioned three models or, for that matter, any of the twenty models, the reader is encouraged to consult the 1996 edition of *Models of Teaching*. For the purposes of this chapter, a brief explanation of the three most commonly used models follows:

1. *Advance Organizer*

The advance organizer model is mistakenly equated with "direct teaching." While they share some theoretical underpinnings, there is a separate model that addresses "direct instruction." Advance organizer involves the refinement of presentations, and as David Ausubel points out in a memorandum to Bruce Joyce in November 1968, "So why not provide the scaffold (of ideas) at the beginning (of the course)? Let the student in on the secret of the structure, including an understanding of how it continually emerges through further inquiry, so that the mind can be active as the course progresses" (265). Indeed, Ausubel is primarily concerned with helping teachers organize and convey large amounts of information as meaningfully and efficiently as possible (267). His model is designed to strengthen students' cognitive structures. Their knowledge of a particular subject at any given time and how well organized, clear, and stable this knowledge is is of primary importance to Ausubel. In other words, cognitive structure has to do with what kind of knowledge a student is able to acquire, and the extent to which this knowledge will be acquired depends upon how well it is organized by the teacher. The syntax of the advance organizer model is as follows:

Phase One
Presentation of advance organizer
- Clarify aims of the lesson
- Present organizer
  - Identify defining attributes
  - Give examples
  - Provide context
  - Repeat
  - Prompt awareness of learner's relevant knowledge and

Phase Two
Presentation of learning task or material
- Present material
- Maintain attention
- Make organization explicit
- Make logical order of learning material explicit experience

Phase Three
Strengthening Cognitive Organization
- Use principles of integrative reconciliation
- Promote active reception learning
- Elicit critical approach to subject matter
- Clarify

2. *Cooperative Learning*

The assumptions that underlie the development of cooperative learning communities are straightforward (1–7 below compiled from p. 68):

1. The synergy generated in cooperative settings generates more motivation than in individualistic, competitive environments. Integrative social groups are, in effect, more than the sum of their parts. The feelings of connectedness produce positive energy.
2. The members of cooperative groups learn from one another. Each learner has more helping hands than in a structure that generates

isolation.
3. Interacting with one another produces cognitive as well as social complexity, creating more intellectual activity that increases learning when contrasted with solitary study.
4. Cooperation increases positive feelings toward one another, reducing alienation and loneliness, building relationships, and providing affirmative views of other people.
5. Cooperation increases self-esteem, not only through increased learning but through the feeling of being respected and cared for by the others in the environment.
6. Students can respond to experience in tasks requiring cooperation by increasing their capacity to work productively together. In other words, the more children are given the opportunity to work together, the better they get at it, which benefits their general social skills.
7. Students, including primary school children, can learn from training to increase their ability to work together.

Interest in cooperative learning has been growing for many years. The more sophisticated research procedures that now exist have enabled better tests of the assumptions and more precise estimates of the effect of cooperative learning on academic, personal, and social behavior (68). An important question to ask is whether cooperative groups do, in fact, generate the energy that results in improved learning, as stated above. The evidence is largely affirmative.

The syntax of cooperative learning is roughly the following (84):

Phase One | Students encounter puzzling situation.

Phase Two | Students explore reactions to the situation.

Phase Three | Students formulate study task and organize for study (problem definition, role, assignments, and so forth).

Phase Four | Independent and group study.

Phase Five | Students analyze progress and process.

Phase Six | Recycle activity.

The teacher's role in group investigation or cooperative learning is one of counselor, consultant, and friendly critic. Of course the teacher must be a facilitator and keep the group focused on the tasks at hand. Many theorists have documented the benefits of cooperative learning (Johnson and Johnson, 1974; Johnson, Maruyana and Nelson, 1981; Slavin, 1983; Hunt, 1971).

3. *Concept Attainment*

Jerome Bruner, previously mentioned in this chapter, is a theorist who has contributed a great deal to our understanding of how categorizing and formulating concepts works (Bruner, Goodnow, and Austin, 1967). Indeed, concept attainment is "the search for and listing of attributes that can be used to distinguish exemplars from non-exemplars of various categories" (233). Derived from Bruner's study of concepts, each term has a special meaning: Exemplars are a subset of a collection of data or a data set. The category is the subset or collection of samples that share one or more characteristics that are missing in the others. It is by comparing the positive exemplars and contrasting them with the negative ones that the concept or category is learned (167–68). Another term that is important in Bruner's lexicon is "attributes." Essential attributes are those that are critical to the domain under consideration. Another important term is "attribute value." This refers to the degree to which an attribute is present in any particular example (168). There are, of course, other key terms that are part and parcel of a full understanding and treatment of this model. The reader is encouraged to refer once again to *Models of Teaching*.

The syntax of the concept attainment model is as follows:

Phase One
Presentation of Data and Identification of Concept
- Teacher presents labeled examples
- Students compare attributes in positive and negative examples
- Students generate and test hypotheses
- Students state a definition according to the essential attributes

Phase Two
Testing Attainment of the Concept
- Students identify additional unlabeled examples as yes or no
- Teacher confirms hypotheses, names concepts, and restates definitions according to essential attributes
- Students generate examples

Phase Three
Analysis of Thinking Strategies
- Students describe thoughts
- Students discuss role of hypotheses and attributes
- Students discuss type and number of hypotheses

During the flow of the lesson, the teacher needs to be supportive of the students' hypotheses and needs to create a dialogue in which students test their hypotheses against one another's (175). Also, concept attainment lessons require that positive and negative exemplars be presented to the students. It should be stressed that the students' job in concept attainment is not to invent new concepts but to attain those that have previously been selected by the teacher (175).

IMPROVING THE QUALITY OF INSTRUCTION

In addition to the excellent and instrumental work in *Models of Teaching*, the topic of instruction has been studied extensively by the prolific writer Allan Glatthorn. He is a very influential figure in Massachusetts education circles and has been contracted by the MASCD (Massachusetts Association for Supervision and Curriculum Development) on several occasions to advise the state education agencies on the best directions for improving curriculum and instruction. Glatthorn believes that the quality of instruction is one of the most important elements in improving learning (1995). While it is generally understood that there is no one way to teach children, there are practices that are more strongly favored than others in terms of evidence in the research literature. For example, the following practices are generally viewed as strongly supported by the research (Glatthorn, 1995):

1. Teachers must make appropriate and effective use of direct instruction. The direct instruction model focuses on the teacher as presenter and manager of learning using some variation of the following model: develops an anticipatory set, models and provides input, provides for guided and independent practice, checks for understanding, and achieves closure. The direct instruction model seems useful for teaching many of the basic skills. (*Author's Note:* The direct instruction model is closely aligned to the advance organizer model previously explained, and both are supported by research evidence and by the practicality of implementation of both models.)
2. Teachers need to nurture in themselves the ability to make appropriate and effective use of a constructivist model. Such a model involves, among other things, activation of prior learning, identification of a contextualized problem to be solved, facilitation of access to generative knowledge, and teaching of learning strategies in subject matter context. (*Author's Note:* The constructivist model is popular in the sense of a long-standing liberal tradition within the education field stemming from the work of Kenneth S. Goodman [1967] and others, and passing through a widespread acceptance of whole language as a methodology for teaching reading and finally within the past decade taking shape as a model called constructivism.)
3. Providing for both group and individual accountability (Slavin, 1990) seems to be a preferred delivery model for cooperative learning. (As noted above, cooperative learning seems to be one of the three most commonly implemented models of teaching.)

4. Teachers need to make effective use of technology. While the research support for the advantages of technology *as a learning medium* is not very well grounded (Glatthorn, 1995), nonetheless it is well known that technology is a fact of life in the twenty-first century, and all students and teachers need to work toward an effective integration of technology with curriculum and instruction.
5. Teachers should group students flexibly in relation to their affective and cognitive needs. Although the research in general supports heterogeneous groupings (Glatthorn, 1995), the issue seems to be more complex than most educators realize. (*Author's Note:* It is the understanding of this author that the debate on heterogeneous versus homogenous grouping continues to be carried out within the public sector especially as this debate relates to achievement levels on standardized, high-stakes testing.)
6. Teachers need ongoing high-quality staff development in order to become more reflective problem solvers. Although teachers need to develop program-specific skills, it may in the long run be more effective to have teachers learn to be effective decision makers and problem solvers.

The above synthesis of what constitutes quality instruction and research-based practice in teaching is in no way intended to be a comprehensive list of effective methods. What is more important is that the above practices have evolved within a dominant context—behaviorism—that made it difficult, if not impossible, to fully realize the potential of the above research-based practices. Now it has been the presumption in this chapter that research-based instructional theory has not made its way into the world of daily teaching and learning. The important point is that within the context of behaviorism, the above research could not flourish and could not emerge successfully to change the face of instructional methodology in the United States. Indeed, as we have seen, of the many sound research-based models, only three have found their way into daily practice.

In a publication of the ASCD (Association for Supervision and Curriculum Development) entitled *Making Connections: Teaching and the Human Brain* (Caine and Caine, 1991), this idea of the behaviorist context is further elucidated:

> The factory model provided fertile soil for the behavioral approach to learning, which has dominated educational practices for the past fifty years It is an approach predicated on the beliefs that what we learn can be reduced to specific, readily-identifiable parts and that equally identifiable rewards and punishments can be used to "produce" the desired learning.

Behavioral approaches, by ignoring the power and vitality of the inner life of students and their capacity to produce personally and intellectually relevant meanings, have interfered with the development of more challenging and fulfilling approaches to learning and teaching. New definitions of behavior have blurred the lines between behaviorism and cognitive psychology. According to Morton Hunt, author of *The Universe Within* (1982): "The wonder of wonders is that so many intelligent and thoughtful people could have believed that behaviorism was an adequate explanation for human behavior" (53). And in their book *Hippocampus as a Cognitive Map*, O'Keefe and Nadel (1978), simply say, "Skinner was wrong." (15)

The authors of *Making Connections* point out explicitly that one of the many problems with the behaviorist approach is that it does not provide for a way to acknowledge invisible consequences. What Renate Nummela Caine and Geoffrey Caine intend by this statement is an emphasis on the fact that teacher behaviors do not have a tight linear connection to student behaviors, that is, each teacher behavior may have vast consequences beyond what might be obvious to the teacher. Similarly, students' behaviors do not necessarily demonstrate a reaction to what the teacher may have done, but, rather, they may be a delayed reaction that represents a kind of consequence that was unintended yet is very real in terms of what is occurring *at that moment* in the learning environment of the classroom.

An additional problem arises in behaviorist thinking when rewards and punishments are considered. The main problem with behavioral S-R-R thinking (learning understood as a series of events: stimulus-response-reward) is that learning outcomes are automatically viewed as resultant actions of the instructional process, which is, as we saw in chapter 5, difficult if not impossible to prove. Also, there is a question about the problematic nature of predetermining the outcomes of instruction, that is, where planning for a lesson is so neatly done that the only outcomes that are acceptable are those that are *intended*. What we know from constructivist thinking, as well as from more recent phenomenological studies, is that there are outcomes that are the product of the instructional moment rather than the product of good planning on the part of a teacher.

Caine and Caine questioned many assumptions that existed about the educational process prior to their undertaking the research for *Making Connections* (1991). Indeed, their "findings" relative to teaching and the human brain were made prior to the beginning of a decade of educational reform laws that did not, generally, incorporate a response to the following dilemma: "The problem is that an overemphasis on output, performance, and the short-term prevents us from really using our brains and maximizing learning. A deep shift in the appreciation of outcomes is needed. We simply must part with the idea that specific pieces of information 'taught' to learners for rewards is an effective use of our brains or theirs. That type of teaching does not work well and does not engage the brain sufficiently. For the shift to occur, we need to seek the patterns that connect. The answer lies in teaching for meaning" (180). This is a fabulous idea. To return to a fundamental notion of teaching that puts the emphasis on "meaning" sounds revolutionary, *is* revolutionary, and has rarely, it seems, been accomplished in the public school system of the United States. Why? There are many reasons, but among them is the undeniable fact that the instructional theories and research results that have been sitting on shelves for more than fifty years must be part of the problem since this situation speaks to a neglect on the part of practitioners who have not accessed the best thinking about teaching and learning available for quite some time. (The reader should understand that this author does not blame teachers for this neglect. Rather, I would put the blame on a dysfunctional system that has not responded to the broader issues that have been brought up in this book regarding how education reform generally has proceeded in directions that have been, at the very least, counterproductive and, at the most, destructive.)

BACK TO THE INSTRUCTIONAL FUTURE

As I attempt to be futuristic in my view of instruction and its role in the reshaping of the educational system, I nonetheless find myself looking over my shoulder at ideas one could—cynically—call traditional or even old-fashioned, yet ideas that have merit and demand our analysis. One such idea comes from the renowned thinker in the field of education, Jacques Barzun, who was mentioned previously in this book as someone who influenced this author by his ideas on curriculum. Now I find myself tempted by his ideas on the role of instruction in the schools.

Let me begin by quoting Barzun's view on the state of reading instruction (1991):

> Here we touch the political and social causes of the whole sad odyssey that has brought America to the condition of being, in the words of Arthur Trace, "a land of semi-literates." The causes are not ignorance, poverty, or barbarist instincts; they are "advanced thinking," love of liberty, and the impulse to discover and innovate. It is from on top—by the action of the literate, the cultured, the philosophical, the artistic—that the common faith in the power of reading as central to Western civilization has been destroyed. . . .
>
> For it is true that none of these looks like the rival goals that sophisticated thought preferred—the free play of fancy, creativeness, and immediate enjoyment; self-expression, novelty, and untrammeled choice in pursuing one's own

thing. These pleasures have been touted in the writings of the best philosophers, artists, and political thinkers, and with impatient contempt of school dullness and rogue learning, educators resolved to emancipate the child and afford him these superior joys.

> The folly consisted, not in wanting the lofty results, but in thinking that they could be reached directly. I have elsewhere defined this fallacy as "preposterism"—seeking to obtain straight off what can only be the fruit of some effort, putting the end before the beginning. It should have been obvious that self-expression is real only after the means to it have been acquired. (25)

Barzun is certainly pointed in his criticism of what can only be construed as a direct attack on the whole language movement and its abysmal failure to rescue the state of reading instruction in the United States. But Barzun is correct in that the ideas of the past in terms of reading instruction, that is, the fact that formation of letters and sounding out "meaning" is fundamental to any long-term skill in the art of reading, is probably no longer debatable, although there are many who will continue to debate this. Indeed, the end—the ability to read—must continue to be the instructional goal. And it does not really matter which model of teaching one selects to accomplish this aim. What does matter is that the result of the instruction causes all students to read and be literate for the rest of their lives.

It would be a mistake for us to lose sight of the fact that the gap, the wide gap, between available research in instruction and actual methods used in teaching subject matter continues to present a rather compelling dilemma for all educators who are involved in the teaching of children. The solution to the closing of the gap is in every way linked to the outcome of the instruction, that is, the selection of method must be an action that is held accountable for the outcomes that we desire in schools, namely having children become compassionate, caring citizens who are literate and who can contribute to the betterment of society and of the world in which we live.

CONCLUSION

I believe that it is healthy that many (including this author) continue to grapple with the dichotomy between the most progressive thinking in instructional theory versus the utilization of very sound, well-tested ideas that continue to be relevant and to contribute positively to desirable learning outcomes. Be that as it may, though, it is no less urgent that we close the gap between what is available in terms of instructional methodology and what is actually utilized in classrooms. If education reform is to really transform teaching and learning in the schools, then it must account for not only the most progressive thinking but also that which has stood the test of time.

CHAPTER 7

ASSESSMENT AS NONSENSE
When Art Tries to Double as Science

AS WE HAVE SEEN IN CHAPTERS 4 AND 5, it is difficult if not impossible to precisely determine the relationship between standardized testing and what is taught in schools. Part of the reason that we cannot determine this relationship goes back to the whole idea of the problematic nature of knowledge itself. We saw, for example, that there were different types of knowledge and that it would be impossible to specify and quantify the accidental knowledge that makes up a large portion of a student's knowledge base.

Indeed, we have seen that reliance on test results has not proven to be the hard science that we had hoped it would become. In fact, over the past fifty years quantitative analysis of cognitive output has failed to describe what it is that schools could do better in terms of the delivery of curriculum (this author's synthesis of education reform data). What we know is that assessment of student learning is a much more complicated process than previously believed. Indeed, when assessment tries to be scientific, it reduces the knowledge a student might have obtained (either in school or outside of school) to an absurdly discrete measurement and thereby takes away any of the texture of the knowledge that was obtained. Critical theorists have long bemoaned the fact that schools have continued the ill-fated pursuit of standardized testing in order to demonstrate school outcomes (Apple, 2000; McLaren, 1998).

Giroux has commented on the deterministic nature of schools in the modernist tradition, and he describes the logical consequences:

> While the logic of public schooling may be utterly modernist, it is neither monolithic nor homogenous, but at the same time, the dominant features of public schooling as we enter the new millennium (twenty-first century) are characterized by a modernist project that has increasingly come to rely upon instrumental reason and the standardization of curricula. In part, this can be seen in the regulation of class, racial, and gender differences through rigid forms of testing, sorting, and tracking. Teaching within this logic is subordinated to the mastery of test skills, and educational outcomes are predicted on the narrow success of test scores. Within this discourse, the concept of education as training dominates schooling, and the overriding purpose of schooling is, in large part, to prepare students "to take their place in the corporate order." (Giroux, cited in Trifonas, 2000, 178)

In this chapter *assessment* will be treated in the contemporary sense of the term as used within the educational enterprise: Learning outcomes are the object of whatever professional activity is used to understand whether students have acquired knowledge. This researcher has spent the better part of the past thirty years trying to understand how to capture educational outcomes within the classroom beyond using paper and pencil tests. Similarly, Vito Perrone, in his introduction to an ASCD publication on assessment (1991), notes that "Student evaluation is basic student growth. It demands careful, thoughtful attention. Yet what typically passes for student evaluation, what fills the public discourse, is an overarching model of assessment, built around a host of standardized tests, that doesn't get particularly close to student learning and doesn't provide teachers with much information of consequence" (vii). I would add to Perrone's statement that assessment that accomplishes getting "close to student learning" is the kind of assessment that has been referred to as *authentic* or *alternative* (in this book and in many other sources). I would also add that authentic assessment is an attempt to deregulate the overpowering and overbearing design offered by psychology to assess student learning. I would also introduce the notion of artfulness in this discussion of assessment because any real understanding of a student's cognitive profile requires an assessment that is characterized by thoughtful analysis of the many complexities that go into teaching and learning within any classroom.

In Perrone's ASCD book on assessment, there is a chapter that is the contribution of a researcher named Kathy Jervis as she recounts her qualitative research conducted within a third-/fourth-grade classroom in New York

City. Jervis observed a classroom taught by a teacher (referred to only as Karen) for an entire school year. As Jervis explicitly states in the opening paragraph, she functioned as a note taker and did not participate in the activities. This ethnographic study revealed many subtleties about life in an urban elementary classroom, not the least of which was the emphasis on doing well on standardized tests. As Jervis concludes in her chapter, "The *New York Times* will print these scores in a front page story, realtors will use them to advise their clients where to live, and university researchers will use them to identify effective schools" (Perrone, 1991, 21).

Let me now take the opportunity to discuss an important distinction made throughout this book. I want to be clear when I talk about assessment as being a preferred art as opposed to a preferred science. It should be noted that quantitative analysis has its place, and there are times when an elaborate description using many and varied statistical tools is a desirable end. Central tendency on the normal bell curve has some validity and has its place when large numbers of subjects or amount of data are being utilized. For example, there are times when NCE (normal curve equivalent) and SD (standard deviation) are a desirable way to report data.

Similarly, this researcher found in gathering standardized test scores on a modestly large population, that is, more than one hundred students per grade, that standardized test data reported as percentile rank (ERB data) could be correlated with other standardized data reported from statewide testing results in Massachusetts (MEAP [Massachusetts Educational Assessment Program] scores and that these correlations were a convenient way to report on the status of a school district's accomplishments in reading and math over a school year. Correlation between the so-called MEAP data (currently called MCAS) and the ERB (Educational Record Bureau) test results could be drawn for certain grades since the population of test takers was controlled and the opportunity for longitudinal analysis, that is, from grades 4 to 5, was also offered because the school district had configured its schools as K–5, 6–8, and 9–12 thereby allowing this researcher to draw some comparisons. As the reader can see in the basic x-y axis analysis in Figure 1, curriculum correlations were drawn for grade 4 reading vis-à-vis ERB testing as compared to MEAP grade 4 reading results. The correlation was found to be extremely high (+.90 to +.95). A conclusion was drawn for the sake of evaluating the reading program in a gross manner (as opposed to a fine analysis) that allowed us to conclude that there was a very strong indicator of curriculum success with our reading programs. Now it should be stated very clearly that no conclusion was ever drawn that these tests were, in fact, matched to the precise reading program implemented in the school district, but it is intriguing and in some ways more *artful* to look at disparate data from different sources, that is, different tests while controlling the subjects, that is, the students, to see whether the *method of analysis* is valid and reliable. In a gross analysis, we were able to conclude that our fourth-grade students were benefiting in general terms from our reading instruction in the school district.

In similar ways, Figure 7.1 shows the same kind of conclusion for math. The ERB math result as compared to the MEAP math result indicates a strong correlation between the performance of our fourth graders in mathematics as measured by two different testing instruments. Now it should be pointed out here that in both cases (reading and mathematics) neither the students nor the teachers were being evaluated. In fact, the students tested in grade 4 with the ERB were a different group of students as those tested using the MEAP, but they were also fourth graders. These kinds of correlations are in some sense an attempt to be artful and creative with data and to use it for an *assessment* as opposed to a straight reporting of results by standardized methodology.

In Figure 7.2, correlations were drawn between MEAP and ERB for eighth graders. We found that the correlation between ERB and MEAP was similarly strong as it was in the case of grade 4. For mathematics it was found to be a less strong correlation, yet it was indeed a fairly strong indicator of curriculum success. Now it is important to note that in all cases these kinds of analysis do not attempt in any way to describe either the curriculum or the test being used to evaluate the curriculum. In fact, what we are trying to do is perform an artful analysis of the performance of a school district in basic subjects such as reading and math. Furthermore, these correlations, while statistically accurate, should only be viewed wholistically.

We could not draw conclusions about either the tests or the students, or the teachers for that matter, since the use of the data is what I would call an *integrated curriculum analysis*, which utilizes data to draw some inferences about the effectiveness of a school or a school program. In this case, in looking at Figure 7.2, the correlation is strong. Yet we find that in the case of mathematics it is slightly less strong than in the case of reading. A gross analysis might lead one to conclude either that eighth graders generally perform better in reading than math or that the teaching of reading is a stronger instructional program than that of mathematics. These conclusions would not be accurate since we are involved here with finding ways to integrate disparate measures across populations and over time in order to gauge the success, generally, of school programs. *It is rare to perform these kinds of artful analyses because: (1) they are not codified in educational research; and (2) they are not widespread in terms of popularity.* However, when we talk about assessment, it is the belief of this author that finding creative ways to use data is more faithful to the notion of authentic assessment than is the straight reporting of numbers generated by standardized testing.

In Figure 7.3, we see a longitudinal study from grades 4 to 5, which is an example of how testing in one year might inform the instructional program the following school year. The longitudinal analysis confirms a progression of school development in grade 4 to grade 5 mathematics. We might even say that this progression is consistent with the expectations of the academic program. In the case of reading, the progression is only slight, yet there does not seem to be any data to indicate a regression of skills; if anything, we would be talking about a maintenance of skills in this case since the correlation is fairly high at +.70 to +.75.

There should be little or no doubt that assessment is a key component of education reform. Indeed, Grant Wiggins and Jay McTighe note that it is possible to "think like an assessor" (1998, 63). My own work in educational theory and curriculum modeling has led me to attempt this kind of approach to theorizing and practicing assessment of student learning. It is my conviction that a wholistic model of assessment might clarify the cognitive profile of the learner as well as aid in decisions of school effectiveness. For any of this to occur, however, it is wise to heed Jerome Bruner's (1996) advice: "As every historian of science in the last hundred years has pointed out, scientists use all sorts of aids and intuitions and stories and metaphors to help them in their quest to get their speculative model to fit 'nature.' . . . They are not just tied to observation and measurement but know how to get around in the theory even without them" (123). As a social scientist, I believe that Bruner's observation helps us justify the use of a wholistic model of assessment and not limit ourselves to standardized measures when we judge either students' learning or overall school or school districts' effectiveness. We might also do well to pay attention, as some testing theorists do, to the issue of morality within assessment (Wiggins, 1993).

WHOLISTIC ASSESSMENT

Wholistic assessment is vested in quality schools kind of thinking. Organizational change strategies are also an important part of any design that claims to be dynamic and wholistic. The quality schools movement of the 1980s and 1990s focused on the use of tools such as pareto charts, cause-effect diagrams, and scatter diagrams to assist in the conceptualization of the *human side* of teaching and learning. It is clear to me now as a social scientist that total quality (or rather quality schools) thinking was an attempt to capture the whole of human communication within the organization called school.

FIGURE 7.1

CORRELATION BETWEEN MEAP AND ERB

CURRICULUM CORRELATIONS (MONITOR EFFECTIVENESS OF COMMON SUBJECT AREAS AS MEASURED BY TWO SEPARATE ASSESSMENTS—MEAP AND ERB) N.B. (NOT THE SAME STUDENTS)

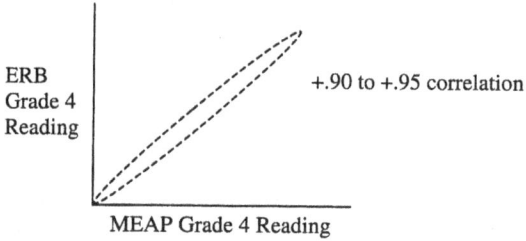

Conclusion: Both results at high end of suburban range. Very strong indicator of curriculum success.

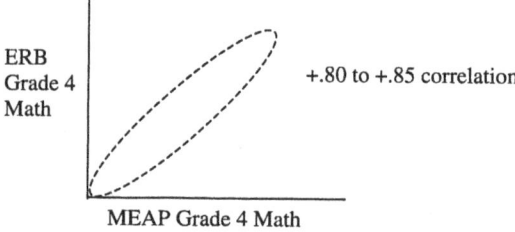

Conclusion: ERB result at high end of suburban range; MEAP result near center of range. Strong indicator of curriculum success.

Assessment as Nonsense 109

FIGURE 7.2

CORRELATION BETWEEN MEAP AND ERB

CURRICULUM CORRELATIONS (MONITOR EFFECTIVENESS OF COMMON SUBJECT AREAS AS MEASURED BY TWO SEPARATE ASSESSMENTS—MEAP AND ERB)

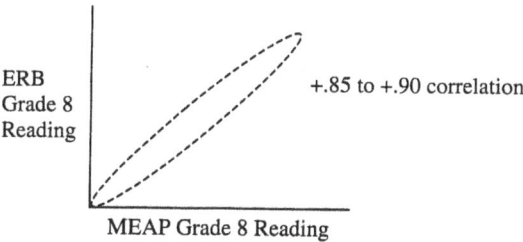

Conclusion: ERB at center of suburban range; MEAP at low end of range. Strong indicator of curriculum success.

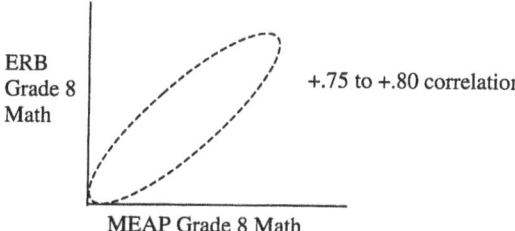

Conclusion: ERB at center of suburban range; MEAP just barely below low end of range. Fairly strong indicator of curriculum success.

FIGURE 7.3

CORRELATION BETWEEN MEAP AND ERB

LONGITUDINAL: GRADE 4 MATH (MEAP) À GRADE 5 MATH (ERB) (SAME STUDENTS)

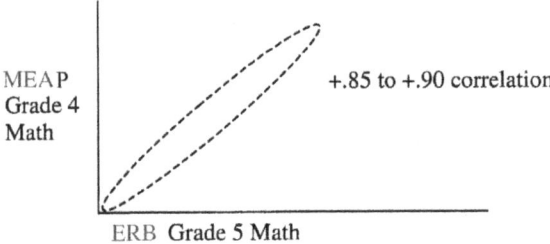

Conclusion: MEAP just below center of range; ERB at low end of range. Consistent progression of skill development.

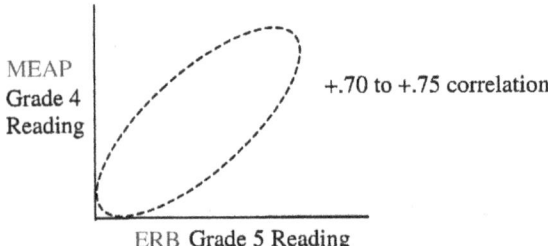

Conclusion: MEAP at high end of range; ERB at low end of range. Maintenance of skills or slight progression.

Admittedly a large and ubiquitous topic, wholistic assessment is nonetheless a very definable one as long as one remembers to demonstrate the kinds of assessment that are possible within schools. If we are focused on the human interaction in schools, we will not be surprised to find that a lot of data can be obtained from the verbal interactions that are part and parcel of the *process* of teaching and learning. And while teaching and learning are surely embedded in a wholistic conceptualization of assessment, we need to remember at all times, nonetheless, that in order to attain the highest level of teaching or learning, assessment must be an integral part of instruction, that is, assessment needs to be thought of as an episode of learning (Wolf, 1990). As one researcher put it in her own inimitably intriguing way, "The frontier in assessment has a different address. It has to do with seizing that third, and unrecognized, aspect of assessment, which is neither measurement, nor simply inculturation, but an occasion for learning" (Wolf, 1990, 4).

This notion of attaining the highest level of integration among teaching, learning, and assessment is reinforced by Lauren B. Resnick, who describes higher order thinking as involving the application of multiple criteria, as demanding self-regulation of the thinking process, and as effortful (1987). What this implies is that assessment cannot be viewed as a terminal event, that is, an event that takes place at the conclusion of instruction. Rather, assessment must be seamless, and it must transcend the usual boundaries ascribed to the usual business of teaching and learning.

Dennie Palmer Wolf explains, in regard to the essential character of assessment, that first and foremost it is of cardinal importance that assessment be conducted as part of ongoing work that students see as meaningful (1990, 8). Furthermore, she notes that coming to an understanding of what is meaningful is, of itself, a part of the instructional process and that excellence is, in fact, a composite idea: It involves diverse aspects of work including know-how, pursuit, force, and accomplishment. And we must be cognizant of the notion of artfulness in that there is a need for *sustained assessment* by which Wolf means "the ongoing appraisal of work over time in a way that allows for both self-assessment or reflection and social assessment or response and critique" (9).

> We know that artists and writers and performers put a high premium on this notion of sustained assessment since there is no opportunity for them to become accomplished in their craft without a boundless series of assessments by a close inner circle as well as by a broader audience of critics. Perhaps it is time to think of the classroom in this way, that is, in order to attain a truly artful assessment it is necessary to understand that we need a broad array of data and of verbal input about the teaching and learning process rather than a simple snapshot of the cognitive profile of each student (that is, paper and pencil tests at the end of instructional units).

The notion of artfulness is an intriguing idea and one that brings up a frequently used tool, over the past decade, to accomplish authentic assessment. What I am referring to is of course the portfolio. Portfolios have been utilized broadly across the United States especially in elementary classrooms as a means to compile and capture a student's work and performance in school. Portfolios have been attempted sporadically in many districts throughout the country as well as attempted by whole states. For example, in Vermont an experiment using portfolio assessment was mandated by law and became part of the instructional program in the early 1990s. The project had an enormous potential for success; however, a study by the Rand Corporation found some problem with the reliability of the assessments that resulted from these portfolios (Rothman, 1992). There seems to have been, according to the Rand study, some serious problems in the areas of rater reliability in scoring the portfolios in that scorers tended to have disagreement about the quality of students' work. In other words, rater reliability, which is an essential part of the validation process of any instrument, could not be established. Now it is important to note that these portfolios must be viewed as product portfolios, that is, the collection of artifacts from student work. Because Vermont tended to implement portfolios in a way that mandated assessments at specific times with specific ratings, these assessments, which had the potential to be authentic, ended up looking more like standardized tests. In fact, the harshest criticism of the whole process was made by a senior social scientist at Rand who determined that the low levels of reliability in the Vermont portfolio process really amounted to a meaningless set of scores. As he put it, "You can't measure anything unless you measure it reliably" (Rothman, 1992, 20).

Contrary to this view of a lack of measurement reliability, it should be clear that a portfolio, in order to be effective, must be more than simply a product of classroom learning tasks. Therefore, the Rand study confirmed what ought to have been clear to all observers in the Vermont experiment, namely that the portfolios themselves took on the quality of standardized tests. Contrary to this view of portfolios, a broader view would allow for both product and process portfolio within the educational setting. Wolf distinguishes between critical items in a process portfolio from those that might be optional. She notes that the following items are to be viewed as essential within a process portfolio (compiled from Wolf, 1990, 35–36):

1. Students should take responsibility for building a developmentally organized sample of their work that requires a chronological collection of writing. Students must routinely collect notes, drafts, reflections, and final versions.

2. Students should be given class time as well as guided instruction time in appraising their own work. This should take the form of questions that students can apply to their writing. Sample reflections might include: choosing a satisfying and unsatisfying piece of work and comment on what makes them different; selecting and commenting on a piece in which the student learned something as a writer; or choosing a piece that the student loves and explaining what the student would like to do in terms of changing it. (*Author's Note:* The social side of appraisal begins with response rather than critique from other readers such as peers and teachers. In these responses, readers pick out for students what they find memorable or worthy of pursuit in their pieces. Readers also indicate moments when they lose the thread, are puzzled, or disinterested.)
3. Students should return to the work of forming a longitudinal sample of their work, that is, students should get used to the idea that a good sample of work is a chronological pursuit.
4. Students should begin to look across their works and ask questions about how they are changing as writers.
5. Students should make a selection from the entire corpus of work available to them in their writing folders in an effort to present the most effective picture of themselves as writers.
6. Students and teachers should review the portfolio discussing where it is successful and where it is still in need of work. Teachers may suggest the inclusion of different pieces of work or pieces of work that could be revised.
7. Students should consider the comments in the portfolios, work on them, and submit them in their final form, and teachers, acting as scorers, should read the portfolios and generate profiles. This data is returned to students, used to evaluate the health of the writing program in the schools, and provides a basis for reports of student writing achievement in the district.

In terms of the *optional items* in a process portfolio, the following are mentioned (Wolf, 35–36).

1. Autobiography of a writer: This might include the kinds of resources that they believe they have as writers, for example, memory, reading, knowledge of another language, and so forth.
2. Research: This might include comparing the writing one does in two different classes and also noting the difference between the writing that is done inside of school as opposed to outside of school.

3. Family review of writing folders: This might include students taking folders home to present them to a member of the family and asking members of the family to respond by writing and recording comments.

It should be clear that our discussion of portfolios and our description of what it is that students do to create these portfolios is inextricably linked to the whole construct of "understanding," that is, the notion of how students come to understand their own work and understand the benchmarks for excellent performance. Now this notion of authentic assessment obliges us to consider in more detail the notion of authenticity. One of the leading researchers in the area of assessment in testing is Grant Wiggins, and he has asked important questions and provided answers. For example, the question of authenticity: "Why is it more than face validity? Why should it be a test design value—irrespective of any correlations that might exist between proposed tests and pre-existing tests? What do we mean by performance, and how will an understanding of it change our conception of competency (and hence validity)? To what extent is validity inseparable from the context in which tests are used?" (Wiggins, 1993, 207).

Some of the answers that Wiggins provides are extensive, but let us simplify this issue by synthesizing some of the main points. First of all, it is important to know that *understanding* is not cued knowledge; performance is never the sum of drills; and problems are not exercises. Wiggins would tell us that mastery is not achieved by the unthinking use of algorithms. He would further explain that "We can not be said to understand something, in other words, unless we can employ it wisely, fluently, flexibly, and aptly in particular and diverse contexts" (207). Put another way, we owe to Wiggins certain insights that we now take for granted about the issue of authentic assessment. One of these issues is the idea that we cannot deconstruct knowledge into discrete elements and then test it and conclude that because of a certain performance on that test that a student understands the concept that was broken down in the first place. Another clarification that we owe to Wiggins is the whole idea of "habit." "Habits by their repetitive nature are not something that can ever be tested by a one-shot test" (207).

Yet Wiggins offers us much more than a simple definitional understanding of key concepts in the area of assessment. He introduces important ideas such as morality, judgment, and context. In other words, the authenticity of assessment depends not only upon the work carried out by students being fluid, seamless, and chronological but also that the work itself that is carried out in the classroom has some larger meaning to student, teacher, and society at large. What this implies for us as educators, and as individuals who wish for

Assessment as Nonsense

a better life for students, is that assessment should be carried out in a moral way and should have features of good judgment. It also should be sensible in terms of the frequency of the episodes of assessment as well as the sequence of how assessment is implemented. Let us examine further some of the just mentioned ideas.

HABIT

When we discuss habit, we normally think of the features of repetitiveness and perhaps issues of accuracy and focus. Yet Wiggins tells us that habit, especially higher-order habit, is "an intelligent proneness, not a reflex" (217).

AUTHENTICITY

Wiggins clarifies what is involved in authenticity when he presents us with the following points (compiled from 1993, 230–31):

1. Engaging and worthy problems or questions of importance, in which students must use knowledge to fashion performances effectively and creatively. The tasks are either replicas of or analogous to the kinds of problems faced by adult citizens and consumers or professionals in the field.
2. Faithful representation of the context facing workers in a field of study or in the real-life "tests" of adult life. The formal options, constraints, and access to resources are apt as opposed to arbitrary. In particular, the use of excessive secrecy, limits on methods, the imposition of arbitrary deadlines or restraints on the use of resources to rethink, consult, revise, and so on—all with the aim of making testing more efficient—should be minimized and evaluated.
3. Nonroutine and multistage tasks—in other words, real problems. Recall or "plugging in" is insufficient or irrelevant. Problems require a repertoire of knowledge and good judgment in determining which knowledge is apt when and where, and skill in prioritizing and organizing the phases of problem clarification and solution.
4. Tasks that require the student to produce a quality product and/or performance.
5. Transparent or demystified criteria and standards. The test allows for thorough preparation as well as accurate self-assessment and self-adjustment by the student; questions and tasks may be discussed, clarified, and even appropriately modified through discussion with the assessor and/or one's colleagues.

6. Interactions between assessor and assessee. Tests ask the students to justify answers or choices and often to respond to follow-up or probing questions.
7. Response-contingent challenges where the effect of both process and product/performance (sensitivity to audience, situation, and context) determines the quality of the results. Thus there is concurrent feedback in the possibility of self-adjustment during the test.
8. Trained assessor judgment, in reference to clear and appropriate criteria. An oversight or audit function exists: There is always the possibility of questioning and perhaps altering a result, given the open and fallible nature of the formal judgment.
9. The search for patterns of response and diverse settings. Emphasis is on the consistency of student work—the assessment of habits of mind in performance.

CONTEXT

Contextual issues, according to Wiggins, relate to test administration itself (239). In other words, test situations are situation specific and do not allow the assessor to perform a *clinical* litmus test of what students have learned in school subjects. Yes, we can try to understand what they "know" through test items, but we will always come up short since the questions themselves are a microcosm of the larger concept being assessed. It is also problematic that the context cannot be assessed, and therefore it is, by definition, an unmeasured part of the entity being assessed. (This author has come to the conclusion on several occasions that student performance is tied to myriad factors that are seemingly unrelated to the assessment of a particular subject matter. In fact, the context has a large amount of influence over whether students can and will perform well: health, disposition to learn, familial situation, emotional state, and so forth.)

In *The Truth about Testing*, W. James Popham puts to rest any doubts that we might have concerning the seriousness of the issues surrounding testing and assessment (2001). He talks about the mystique surrounding standardized testing (37) and offers several reasons for being skeptical about any sound educational use of the results of this kind of testing.

The first reason that Popham provides has to do with the mismatch between teaching and testing. While this seems obvious to most educators and, in fact, to most well-intentioned and thinking individuals in the general population, it ought to be emphasized here, because it is a forgotten problem due to the frenzy of testing. The political implications are real, as are the consequences for schools (that is, naming schools as underperforming or failing and/or closure of schools by state or federal agencies). Popham states explicitly that "Half or more of what's tested wasn't supposed to be taught in a particular district or state" (43).

The second reason that we need to have healthy skepticism around standardized testing and the use of its results has to do with the fact that what teachers *do* teach well will end up *eliminated* eventually from the test due to what's called high P-value (that is, the percentage of students getting a particular question right). Popham is highlighting a travesty here, namely "standardized achievement tests should not be used to evaluate the quality of students' schooling because the quest for wide score spread tends to eliminate items covering important content that teachers have emphasized and students have mastered" (48).

It seems reasonable to me then to summarize Popham's contribution to this issue of testing and assessment by concluding that we should never judge the quality of a school or an educational program by the results of standardized testing. What we should be doing of course is looking for multiple measures (authentic assessment) that, as previously stated in this chapter, accomplish the goal of capturing the multiplicity of data and evidence that will fairly, accurately, and humanely advance the progress of students in the educational system, allow them to be successful as learners, and permit the possibility of a life that is full of meaningful interactions, fruitful work and noteworthy accomplishments.

Should the reader still be skeptical about whether we need to move toward a more artful approach to the assessment of student learning, let us continue by citing some other important pieces of information that Popham offers us (2001). As it turns out, SES (socioeconomic status) is a significant and influential variable in testing and assessment. This should not be a surprise to anyone who understands that our quest for equity in educational programming has failed because we have a society with stratified economic conditions and multiple cultures and ethnicities coming together in a confused and chaotic world that values the reductionist approach, the efficient approach to judging the quality of education. SES bias in testing is a serious problem. Popham has identified that, at a minimum, the percentage of items judged to be linked to socioeconomic status is as follows (65):

SUBJECT	% SES ITEMS
Reading	15%
Language Arts	65%
Mathematics	5%
Science	45%
Social Studies	45%

In addition to the above bias, Popham identifies a certain percentage of items that were judged to be linked to inherited academic aptitudes. This is an interesting analysis since he introduces a variable that has been controversial for the better part of the past century and that continues to haunt us since it is believed to be a dominant factor as students enter school. Yet it is also believed to be mallable in terms of a longitudinal approach to increasing a person's performance. I am, of course, referring to *aptitude*. What Popham found is the following (73):

SUBJECT	% INHERITED ACADEMIC APTITUDE ITEMS
Reading	40%
Language Arts	35%
Mathematics	20%
Science	55%
Social Studies	50%

Last, but by no means least, Popham gives another compelling reason why we should not use standardized test results. The reason is truistic and ought to have been transparent for many years, but much to the chagrin of virtually everyone involved in the schooling process this reason has been neglected:

> Standardized achievement tests should not be used to judge the quality of students' schooling because factors other than instruction also influence students' performance on these tests. (74) *(The reader is also reminded of chapter 5: fundamental versus accidental knowledge.)*

Let me now anticipate and sort out for the reader a quagmire that may develop around the whole issue of assessment. Popham's work is very revealing and helpful in that it allows us to step back and take a hard look at the variables that *do* impact the eventual outcomes of schooling. Now there are two implications here. There is, first of all, the quality of an entire school program. And there is, of course, the individual achievement of each and every student. Authentic assessment addresses the individual student as opposed to finding large-scale, conglomerate, aggregated data that will support decisions about the health or future of a particular school. Both of these issues are critical to our moving toward a world that will recognize finally the interrelationship between success of students in school and the quality of life we all experience in society at large. This issue (success) will be taken up in more detail in chapter 8. But for now let us try to conclude our discussion of assessment and the artful nature of assessment.

CONCLUSION

We have attempted in this chapter to show that assessment has been misguided in that it has focused too much on standardized testing and too little on authentic analysis of student learning. We have also attempted to show that the *conclusions* drawn from standardized testing are harmful to the overall health and welfare of schools. Now these points, while they cannot be proven to everyone's satisfaction since it is precisely the selection of variables and factors that determines the kinds of conclusions one can draw, it is nonetheless important to note that even some of the most conservative researchers, for example Andrew Porter and Mitchell Chester have admitted that "The assessment and accountability programs should be fair and . . . a fair assessment and accountability program must also include tests that are reliable and valid for the ways in which they are used" (2002, 287). While these researchers do a respectable job of outlining the technical kinds of analyses that are needed in order to verify the reliability and validity of tests, they nonetheless miss a critical point that this author has tried to emphasize throughout this book on education reform: We will never be able to develop, no matter how hard we try, and no matter how much science we utilize in so doing, assessment instruments which will, by themselves, satisfactorily provide the kind of information we need to help students achieve success in school. What we might understand intuitively and may never be able to articulate scientifically is that assessment of the whole child in the learning situation of schools requires time, effort, painstaking attentive analysis, love, compassion, and most of all a desire to see each and every student approach the possibility of achieving a good, focused, and meaningful life due in part to the humanistic educational practices experienced in schools.

PART III

DECIPHERING
THE JARGON
Calling upon Good Sense and Pragmatism

CHAPTER 8

A CULTURAL STUDY OF SUCCESS

AS WE HAVE SEEN IN PREVIOUS CHAPTERS, education reform is not merely a matter of adding up the scores on tests and deciding from the results what direction to take in order to improve the school systems in the United States. Rather, the complexity of teaching and learning requires an encompassing reform strategy that must be tightly linked to the realities of the cultural context in which teaching and learning take place. In this chapter, we will explore the nature of *success* and attempt to shed some light on the sociocultural dimensions of success.

We know that children in most societies attend school for a certain number of years before entering more advanced study in college or in a specialized school or immediately entering the world of work. It is not beyond reason to surmise that the goals and experiences of children around the world must vary greatly. Indeed, the culture in which a child grows up will most assuredly determine how the child views the idea of success, or even the requirements for survival in a highly complicated and precarious world. Now we know that children rely heavily on parents and other significant adult figures to guide them in their pursuit of their goals and aspirations. For some children, a college education is the goal; yet for others, basic literacy is the most that they can hope to accomplish. However, with the growth of industry, trade, and international business, demands for an educated workforce are now commonly heard around the world (Altbach, 1991).

Sociology, and more specifically the sociology of education, is a field that has particular interest in how the educational systems across cultures function to determine the options, as well as the boundaries, that are presented by the sociocultural context in which a child learns, grows, and develops. There are many and varied themes involved in the sociology of education, but one that stands out involves comparative studies in education:

1. Most countries require that students attend school to the age of 16. (Some countries even provide free education for university study for those who qualify.)
2. Educational systems around the world vary widely, but there are also similarities (Boli, Ramirez, and Meyer, 1985).
3. Variations in countries are characterized significantly by differing economic systems whereby wealth and poverty play a central role. Also, educational systems reflect the economic and political institutions of a given country.
4. Sociologists have attempted to trace the origins of modern school systems and, while there are differences of a significant nature in the curricula that have evolved over time, some findings support a greater emphasis on the convergence of curricular themes across nations (Ramirez and Boli-Bennett, 1987). Of course, many researchers question whether the existence of a curricular common thread, internationally, is good news for contemporary society.
5. Some educational theorists interested in the sociology of education question whether the curriculum itself serves the needs of the poor since, for the most part, curriculum programs seem to support and perpetuate a middle-class society. A graphic example of this is the case of developing countries where the poor are taught a curriculum that does not in any way match their life circumstances (Freire, 1972).
6. It is widely acknowledged that race, class, and gender all affect what chances a child has to achieve in school (King, 1999).
7. The NAEP (National Assessment of Educational Progress) compares scores of children around the world in literacy, mathematics, science, and so forth. It is also widely known that these rankings (that is, the test results) provide information on the similarities, differences, and effects of development on educational systems.

While the above analysis evolves from a comparative study of school systems worldwide, and reinforces the notion of a cultural context of success, it is useful to consider how *cultural reproduction* further defines and situates *culture* in the context of a sociological concern for eliminating educational failure, which has been a major concern of this book.

Let us begin by defining what cultural reproduction means. Indeed, a central problem that needs to be examined is the way in which the production and reproduction of knowledge in the curriculum function to control students in explicit ways. Furthermore, the inexplicable yet undeniable existence of a hidden curriculum that dominates teaching and learning in most schools speaks to the organization of subject matter disciplines in ways that are predetermined and foretell the success and failure of students prior to their beginning their school lessons. Therefore, a major focus of this chapter will be the exploration of cultural reproduction and how this reproduction functions in a conceptualization of success that is functional and operational.

We might add that the Durkheimian tradition forces us to examine a particular emphasis on the ways in which moral and symbolic control combine with cultural reproduction in creating a specific schooling experience (Thompson, 2002). Especially noteworthy is Basil Bernstein's focus on the relationship between various educational styles and the school's social order as well as its forms of social control and how this relationship functions within the tradition of cultural reproduction (Bernstein, 1971, 1975). Or equally relevant are Pierre Bourdieu's ideas that, while complementary to Bernstein's and to the Durkheimian orientation, provide insights into the structural context of culture and schooling (Bourdieu, 1977). For our purposes the examination of the role of culture as a legitimate player in the success or failure of students in schools should be a logical and reasonable activity given the evidence supplied in this book concerning the failure of education reform in the United States. The question of whether any such reform has failed or succeeded worldwide is beyond the scope of this chapter and this book. Nonetheless, it can be inferred, given the interconnectedness of economy and culture, that the United States, in its failure of the educational system, creates an unfortunate ripple effect throughout the world. It should be said that there are attempts to improve upon educational systems throughout the world whether these attempts are legislated and enacted.

To continue our examination of the cultural context of schooling, let us consider some of the principal ideas of the three sociologists just mentioned: Durkheim, Bernstein, and Bourdieu.

ÉMILE DURKHEIM

Émile Durkheim devoted his life to the field of sociology in France. He is best known for his focus on four intellectual treatises dealing with labor, sociological methods, suicide, and the elementary forms of religious life. But, for our purposes, perhaps the most significant contribution that Durkheim made deals with influence on the French educational system to incorporate the findings of sociology into its theory and practice. The academic world is undoubtedly indebted to him for his seminal ideas that shaped the worldwide excitement in the field of sociology. For example, his notion of anomie, or rootlessness, normlessness, reflects an absence of recognized and positively accepted norms to regulate action (Thompson, 2002). (That is, the anomic division of labor occurs when norms regulating activities break down or fail to emerge.)

Indeed, a source of this so-called anomie exists where there is discrepancy between a group's expectations and its achievements (Thompson, 2002, 85). It is not difficult to extrapolate then, from this idea of anomie, that a child's cultural understanding of success must be embedded in all of the stimuli and influences on the child throughout his or her developmental years. Furthermore, what is known as "acute economic anomie" forces us to explain failure in terms of a disconnect between the reasonably formed expectations of the child (that is, what the child has been led to believe is possible in his or her life) and the more naturalistic occurrence whereby attainable goals are well out of reach. Surely, in Durkheim's understanding, a disequilibrium is created, a feeling of hopelessness sets in (and suicide rates go up), and the outlook for the future in terms of a positive outcome of success caused by schooling becomes less and less likely, not only because of the previously mentioned disconnect, but also because "the formulation of an appropriate morality for modern society could only proceed after the lessons had been learned about how morality had functioned in relation to previous social structures" (Thompson, 2002, 161). In other words, the relative permanency of the disconnect, given its inextricable link to previously established rules, obviates any realistic renewal or rebuilding of a new moral code that will accommodate and match the expectations of a new generation. Durkheim clarifies this idea when he writes:

> Education is the influence exercised by adult generations on those that are not yet ready for social life. Its object is to arouse and to develop in the child a certain number of physical, intellectual, and moral states which are demanded of him by both the political society as a whole, and the special milieu for which he is specifically destined. . . . It follows from [this] definition . . . that education consists of a methodical socialization of the young generation. (Durkheim, 1956, 370)

And this idea is clarified further by Durkheim's comments on educational change:

> It may well happen that at great intervals a person emerges whose ideas and aspirations go beyond those of his fellows; but isolated individuals are not enough to remake the moral constitution of peoples . . . besides, even though, through some incomprehensible miracle a pedagogical system were constituted in opposition to the social system, this very antagonism would rob it of all effect. If the collective organization whence comes the moral state it is desired to combat is intact, the child is bound to feel its effect from the moment he first has contact with it. The school's artificial environment can protect him only briefly and weakly. To the extent that real life increasingly takes possession of him, it will come to destroy the work of the teacher. *Education, therefore, can be reformed only if society itself is reformed.* To do that, the evil from which it suffers must be attacked at its sources. (Durkheim, 1956, 373) (emphasis added)

The above citation from Durkheim's work is notable for at least two reasons: (1) the above reflections on education reform were made almost fifty years ago; and (2) his sociocultural perspective was France. Any discussion of Durkheim's work—a substantial and extremely influential body of work—must recognize the international perspective that he brought to the discussion of the sociology of education. It has been the premise of this author that a macroperspective on reform has to be the very first agenda item for any lasting change.

BASIL BERNSTEIN

Basil Bernstein offers yet another perspective in the sociology of education by focusing on linguistics and language acquisition. Bernstein was influenced by Durkheim's work and it is widely recognized that Durkheim's insights provided a starting point for Bernstein's theories, which included Durkheim's work on the division of labor, on education, and on symbolic classification. For our purposes I will comment on Bernstein's sociolinguistic contributions as well as his overall impact on education reform.

Bernstein constructed a sociolinguistic theory that, based on observations of British youth and young adults, was a two-part description of language use: He wrote about two codes, one being *restricted,* the other, *elaborated*. Restricted code use for Bernstein was the mark of the lower-class youth in London, and what he learned through his observations was that restricted language use foretold of educational and academic difficulties in school due to the mismatch between the language use of the learner and that of the teacher. In contrast, elaborated code use was found largely among upper-class students, and the match between code use of the learner and of the teacher allowed for a smoother and more seamless articulation as well as communication within the walls of the schools.

Some of Bernstein's other notions that have proven to be significant are the following (1971, 1975):

1. *Differentiating Rituals*
Status within a group (age, gender, housing) is possible because of rituals (habits and social mores), and they provide the basis for academic and social stratification in the school.

2. *Stratified School Structures*
Age, gender, IQ, as well as other attributes provide strong binding categories that are reinforced by the hierarchy within a school as well as the general adult-regulated society outside of school.

3. *Differentiated School Structures*
Within schools, attributes are viewed frequently as in the process of developing, that is, they can be achieved. In terms of rituals, unlike the case of stratified school structures, attributes are pupil generated.

4. *Mechanical Solidarity*
When individuals share a common system of beliefs, social integration arises out of these similarities and social roles are assigned. In other words, the "natural" conduct and behavior of individuals is a direct result of this common belief sharing.

5. *Organic Solidarity*
When individuals relate to each other through a complex interdependence arising from specialized social functions, social integration relies upon the development of *differences* between individuals, and social roles are achieved.

What might be Bernstein's major contribution to American educational thought resides most probably within the realm of sociolinguistics. However, his ideas on schooling paint a picture of education reform etched in social class and social stratification with very little room for dramatic change without a concomitant change in society. Thus *success* ends up being a function more of one's position within socioeconomic stratifications and is reinforced by other individuals who share one's attributes and characteristics. Schools may continue to try to improve learning outcomes for disadvantaged youth, but all of their efforts are at odds with the more prevalent and much more powerful societal features and events.

PIERRE BOURDIEU

Like Bernstein, Bourdieu demonstrates a Durkheimian view of culture, yet there are significant differences. For Bourdieu the family is a key and ever-present source of cultural reinforcement for the child, whereas in Bernstein's work, the broader social fabric and context end up being more significant. SES (socioeconomic status) of the child is viewed by both theorists to be a critical variable in the success or failure of a student in school. However, failure in school (that is, a lack of success) is more predictable in Bourdieu's thinking based on social class than it is for Bernstein who examines the structural context within which schools, society, and family function in the life of the child.

Bourdieu's ideas are best understood in relationship to the work of Bernstein and Durkheim. What can be generalized from the work of all three theorists, and that is most helpful to our discussion now of the cultural study of success, is the fact that education not only transmits culture through academic programming but also that the complexity of curriculum, instruction, and evaluation becomes blurred and defies any simple analysis. Put another way, a child's success or failure in school is more dependent upon the ability to internalize the collective cultural artifacts around him or her than it is a question of pure intellectual and cognitive stature.

To continue our discussion of a cultural context for the idea of success, let us now consider the relationship between cultural context and moral leadership. The reason that we need to focus on this kind of connection is precisely because it has become all too clear over the past decade that the moral decay and value-empty academic programming has created a situation where the moral dimensions of teaching have been all but abandoned. What is left within schools are cultural diversity and a propensity to continue the reproduction of society at large without any consideration for the ultimate results in terms of the quality of life that citizens experience.

Let us explore the idea of the morality of cultural representation a bit further. Cary A. Buzzelli and Bill Johnston provide an explanation that speaks to an understanding of cultural representation as "the images, archetypes, or even stereotypes of identity with which students are labeled" (Harklau, 2000, 37, cited in Buzzelli and Johnston, 2002). They extend Harklau's definition to include not just institutional labels but also ways in which "other cultures" are represented in curricular materials—that is, how representations of these cultures are enshrined in the content of teaching and learning (2002, 97–98). While the authors focus more on cultural representation in terms of its adequacy within the curriculum, what this author finds more intriguing is the question that they ask about these representations, namely: What is the moral significance of the way cultures are represented, misrepresented, or not represented at all by curricular materials (98)?

Indeed, cultural representation is a problematic concept with which to grapple, but when one adds the idea of morality, it becomes even more complex, and rightly so. This author has been and continues to be interested in whether success as defined within a cultural context of schooling has any chance of being improved by legislated education reform. It should be clear to the reader by now that this author would resoundingly answer, "No," to this question. Now the issue for all of us is whether we will be able to change the moral leadership within the context of schooling (and within the context of multiple cultural representations) and arrive at some sort of compromised milieu within schools where teaching and learning can play out in ways that produce less human suffering, more nobility, more compassion, and a quality of life that is acceptable to all.

Buzzelli and Johnston explore the moral dimensions of teaching in curriculum by demonstrating a variety of scenarios where various countries are misrepresented within the curriculum in the United States. While, to an extent, this is a useful approach to cultural representation, it does not go far enough in terms of moral leadership. The authors acknowledge that "the relationship between culture and identity is highly complex" (105). They note that many scholars in fields such as anthropology and cultural studies have become wary to continue the debate on what exactly *culture* is. In fact, they note that *identity* and *culture* have become somewhat synonymous terms and whether they are indeed alike, the concept of identity is at the heart of the moral dilemma inherent in the idea of culture (105). Let us examine further how identity relates to the concept of success. The authors cite Sandra Cisneros's *The House on Mango Street* to illustrate a point:

> The teachers have difficulty pronouncing her name or didn't want to try. I can definitely relate to that. One time, a woman asked me my name, and I told her. She responded, "Well, I can't pronounce that, so I'll just call you 'girl.'" To me, it was not her inability to say my name; it was her lack of effort to say my name, like it was unimportant, like I was. My name means "beautiful flower, richly endowed." I am proud of that. I've tried to live up to that name. It really hurt when she didn't note that the name was unique, ask me its meaning, or even try to say it. If you can't take the time to get to know my name, how can you get to know me? (111)

If identity is closely associated with culture, then success is inextricably linked to one's view of oneself. This is more than just an idea; it is a universal truth that one's identity is what shapes the ultimate result of one's attempts to be successful in life. If this sounds simplistic, it is actually just the opposite.

Cultural representation, now what we can call cultural identity, is a highly complex construct that has been studied extensively by psychologists and sociologists as well as anthropologists, political scientists, and others. Most if not all agree that, in today's world, "what makes teaching a moral activity is, to a significant degree, the social negotiation among its participants" (Buzzelli and Johnston, 2002, 121).

While this author would agree that the negotiation is realized "through the design of curricula, the implementation of lessons, and the exercise of student evaluation and assessment procedures" (121), I would certainly wish to take this moral activity out of the realm of negotiation. Now it should not be interpreted by the reader that I am advocating some sort of moral absolutism. Rather, I advocate a common understanding that if we are to transcend the cultural limitations of success in school as explained by Durkheim, Bernstein, Bourdieu, and others then it seems crucial and extremely timely that we return to a universal notion of morality in order to equalize the possibility of success in school. Equal opportunity to have success in school must be dependent upon a shared sense of what it means to be a moral person and to not be afraid to be a role model of this particular moral entity.

In *Language, Culture, and Teaching: Critical Perspectives for a New Century,* Sonia Nieto defines a successful teaching program, relating to the preparation of new teachers, as being linked to one's professional ability to get to know one's students rather than simply to work on methodology and technique (Nieto, 2002). The author is squarely focused on multiculturalism, diversity, and bilingual education, yet her emphasis is on the fact that language, literacy, and culture are critical components that must be emphasized in teacher preparation programs. Nieto does not specifically define her recommendations in terms of moral leadership, but she implies that the problems within the educational system do not relate simply to teaching and learning but rather to society at large (19).

In terms of cultural identity, Nieto suggests that teachers need to respect students' identities and learn more about them if they are to be effective leaders in a classroom. And if we are reticent to step over the line into the realm of morality, we can take consolation and comfort in the fact that the brilliant Russian psychologist Lev S. Vygotsky acknowledges that "Even our private thoughts and language are originally shaped through the ways we learn to interact with others" (1978, 28). Put simply, our identity, whether viewed in cultural or purely psychological terms, is always shaped and reshaped by how others view us. Whether we are in school or carrying out our lives, there is no doubt that if we are a social being—a successful one—there must be some universal, moral leadership that pervades the educational system and allows for a definition of success that is accessible to all. In this way, the problematic presented by a cultural study of success forces us to reexamine how we might accomplish any goals within the educational system while at the same time preserving a sense of morality acceptable to most reasonable people. These are not pleasant choices, but they must be made. I recommend that we revise, and revive, teaching and learning to include the following:

A FOCUS ON MORAL JUDGMENT RATHER THAN MORAL OUTCOME

1. Engage students in moral dilemmas that force a decision that pits right against wrong, good against evil.
2. Focus students' attention on the reasons that force them to make one choice over another.
3. Engage students in a discussion on how these kinds of decisions might be made so that most of the time they will choose the right course of action (phronesis) and/or the good.
4. Emphasize to children that there are social consequences for every decision or choice.

For most people, moral judgment is the key underlying functionality involved with making choices that end up contributing to a fulfilling and successful life. Therefore, it would be wise to frame the issue of a cultural basis for morality within the context of a more self-centered, identity-bound explanation for why good moral choices are so critical to one's eventual success.

It must be emphasized that the concept of success defies convenient stereotypes and resists simple characterization. As we have seen, our discussion has required a cultural perspective on what it means to be successful. And, it should be added, education reform has attempted not only to legislate what students should know, how they will be tested on what they know, but also has attempted to redefine success in a homogenized way that has robbed most students of any cultural identity that might have been nurtured in a school environment. We can dismiss education reform at this point in time since the minimum competency defined by legislated reform acts has always been the least successful outcome that anyone could design or define. We saw in chapter 2, for example, that the minimum score to succeed on the MCAS (Massachusetts Comprehensive Assessment System) was a score of 220 in a range of possible scores between 200 and 280. This is hardly what I would call success. Furthermore, the harsh reality of bureaucratized school improvement, or education reform, is that legislated, predetermined measures of successful outcome in learning a communalized body of knowledge are almost always the least significant indicators of how schools—teachers and students—have performed.

How might we assist students in making moral decisions? One approach involves developing a hierarchy of values so that when there is a conflict a person can refer to the hierarchy for guidance. One way to accomplish this is "to place God and religious values at the top of the hierarchy, values surrounding character traits such as honesty and benevolence, in an intermediate position, and material values at the bottom of the hierarchy. Thus, when there is a conflict between, for example, acquiring wealth and pursuing the religious life, one can refer to the hierarchy and decide in favor of the religious life" (Rich, 1968, 103). But John M. Rich admits that the hierarchy approach to values and moral choices/decision making relies to an extent upon "things [being] valued not in the abstract, but in relation to particular situations" (104).

Now it is beyond the scope of this chapter to develop a full moral blueprint, as it were, for guidance in decision making. Even though we have all been inculcated with certain values that we have obtained from our families, society, religion, and other sources, it is still true that we prefer sometimes to leave the decision to a broader concern, namely to act morally in concert with the values shared by our own community. This fact of placing the onus of a moral decision on our environment leads us to shift the responsibility for consequences away from ourselves. This is not really a cowardly act, but rather it is one that is based strongly in our instinct for survival. However, to be *successful* requires more independent, courageous action on our part.

CONCLUSION

A study carried out by the researchers Benjamin Levin and J. Anthony Riffel examined the ways in which school systems try to understand and manage social change (Bascia and Hargreaves, 2000, 178). A major premise of the study is an understanding that the strongest impetus for change in schools resides in the larger social environment; "the nature of schooling and the work of teachers are far more powerfully affected by changes in families, in the economy, in law, or in technology than they are by any number of curriculum revisions or school board policies" (178). Furthermore, "although understanding social change is a vital organizational task, it is not easily accomplished" (Levin, 1993, cited in Bascia and Hargreaves, 2000, 179). Also, "a substantial literature in education points to the difficulties in creating meaningful and lasting change" (Cuban, 1990; Sarason, 1996, cited in Bascia and Hargreaves, 2000, 179).

What is clear from Levin and Riffel's study is that change continues to be an elusive commodity in terms of education reform and of creating the kinds of permanent improvements we seek for all children in school. Indeed, the researchers conclude that "A fundamental obstacle to coping with change lies in the tyranny of the standard model of schooling. The educators . . . could see clearly the limits of current practice but could not always see what else they might do. It was as if they recognized that the boat they were in was listing badly, but had nothing else to turn to. . . . Although conditions vary greatly from locale to locale, schooling everywhere looks much the same. Dramatic changes in communications patterns, information handling, and human interaction will need to be reflected in quite different ways of organizing our institutions. It seems evident to us that schools designed for the conditions of the nineteenth century will not do justice to educational needs in the twenty-first century" (2000, 193). If Levin and Riffel are correct and schooling everywhere looks much the same, we can also begin to assume that outcomes of schooling worldwide, in terms of success, experience similar problems. There are no easy solutions and there are even fewer good questions to ask as we grapple with enormous, complex dilemmas in the twenty-first century.

A cultural study of success leads this author to the very unsettling conclusion that education reform, as it has been carried out over the past decade, has failed to respond to the ever-pressing problems that society is presenting to us. What is more, we will almost certainly have to look to past practices that were successful and have been abandoned. It will be necessary to call upon multiple perspectives (tap into all reasonable disciplines and knowledge bases) and most likely engage in what will be developed in chapter 9: a prudent use of reinvention. And this author will dare to use the term *good sense* and will not reject a pragmatic approach to improving the lives of all children and adults who desperately need to be rescued from more than a decade of education reform movements that have paralyzed our nation's schools and polarized virtually all important stakeholders to whom we must look for any hope of reversing the unmistakably downward spiral of schooling so obvious to many.

We have, for far too long, tried to blame the victim, that is, students, for what is to many so obviously located squarely in a sociocultural and political context that determines the distribution of knowledge, cultural capital, and power long before students even enter the schoolhouse (McLaren, 1998; Bernstein, 1975; Apple, 1990).

CHAPTER 9

FROM PANACEAS TO MULTIPLE PERSPECTIVES AND PRUDENT USE OF REINVENTION

OVER THE PAST DECADE, education has been the focus of intense public scrutiny and debate. We have seen in all previous chapters of this book that education reform has undergone a rather surprising period of remarkable inability to improve the schools in the United States. Yet the interest in education as a national agenda item continues unabated. Indeed, there is no sign that the vetted reviews of education reform agendas and platforms will do anything other than continue at a furious and frenzied pace. Prior to 1990 there was polite interest in schools; since 1990 the general public has increasingly paid attention to devastating financial implications, over a lifetime, of not having necessary knowledge and skill to be a productive member of society. It is all too clear to virtually everyone today that if we do not already understand the undeniable importance of education, we are all about to enter a new era of intense, unforgiving public demand that our schools perform nothing less than a miracle.

Buoyed by the barrage of low test scores (or at least scores that show a flat curve over time) reported, it seems, almost daily, and by a series of tragic, violent incidents in schools over the past decade, politicians have seized the moment to garner support for all sorts of policies, platforms, and reforms. Charter schools, voucher systems, school choice—to name the most prominent—have become the call to arms for all disgruntled employers and business executives who were able to appeal to parents' fears that the public educational system had permanently gone amok.

In this chapter I will tender a judgment on education reform efforts in the United States since the early 1990s and will declare legislated reform acts to have failed to accomplish what they intended in the first place. Then, I will describe specific reform programs that have been attempted and have also failed to deliver a redeemed educational system. Finally, I will demonstrate that the continued confusion in American public education makes it mandatory that we focus on a much more radical (that is, root or core knowledge; essence) approach in order to hope to begin the process of eliminating widespread educational failure. In other words, I will try to demonstrate that, by moving away from panaceas and toward multiple perspectives within core knowledge, we might begin to reverse the trend (too long evident) of accepting a political solution that has shown itself to be doomed to failure. In the final analysis I will suggest the prudent use of reinvention, that is, wise use of "new" models of change *and* of multiple perspectives, that is, tapping the knowledge of *all* disciplines that are relevant to education reform (economics, philosophy, psychology, political science, sociology).

THE AGONY WITHOUT ECSTASY

In his incisive and insightful 2003 review of two recent books on the topic of school reform, Zeus Leonardo offers the reader a brief synthesis of some of the major philosophical guideposts of reform in the past decade and then goes on to analyze the major themes of the two books. The title of his review, "The Agony of School Reform: Race, Class, and the Elusive Search for Social Justice," epitomizes the general feeling among many educators, parents, and others about how gauche and ill advised so many reform packages tend to be. School reform (unlike education reform, the topic of this book) can be traced back to the 1980s when the central doctrine of efficiency dominated school reform effort. As Leonardo points out, "Central to the doctrine of efficiency is the breakdown and standardization of knowledge into discrete parts, not only to control the learning process but also to make evaluation of learning outcomes more precise and positive" (37). He goes on to say that "decades of efficiency failed to level the playing field" and that school reform in the 1980s resorted to a structural approach that attempted to "ameliorate the persistent problem of uneven student development between social groups" (37). Leonardo cites Jeannie Oakes's early work on tracking as one example of the restructuring effort that, as he points out, failed. A second wave of school reform known as "reculturation" was attentive to the problem of belief systems and meanings that undergird school practices and remain long after structures have changed (Gitlin and Margonis, 1995, in Leonardo, 2003). And the third and current wave according to Leonardo (37) is squarely fixed on the problem of ideology. It is beyond the scope of this book to challenge Leonardo's assertions about school reform, but let us leave it at the following conclusion: Education reform as a legislated act occurred in the 1990s when matters of ideology became a critical issue in the national debate on public education. In other words, school reform was a microamelioration effort (school by school), whereas education reform was, and still is, focused on the macrolevel, that is, on the improvement of public schooling in America.

The two books reviewed by Leonardo both represent his interdisciplinary approach to school reform. Thus I have selected to comment on these reviews because the ideas that he utilizes, and the focus on the ideological dimension, are very important not only because many failed programs have been attempted in the name of a specific ideology but also because the future of reform will sit squarely in a less ideological context if it is to succeed at all.

The two books reviewed by Leonardo, *Education and Democratic Theory* by A. Belden Fields and Walter Feinberg, and *The Color of School Reform* by Jeffrey R. Henig et al., represent an interdisciplinary approach to school reform. It is precisely for this interdisciplinary approach that this author has referenced Leonardo's review: Both of these books offer renewed advice that a broader, multiple perspectives approach is needed if indeed we are to continue to carry out education reform in a macrocontext. Leonardo points out, rightfully so, that equality of education has been a goal for quite a long time and one that education reform, as well as school reform, has largely ignored. In this sense, the foundation of education reform in terms of equity goes back at least to the days of John Dewey and his push for a democratic education for all students (1916). Furthermore, Leonardo concludes with both a synthesis and a calling to future action. He states that both contemporary books "break new ground on what it means to incorporate ideology critique into school reform" (43). He goes on to say that "Both books conceptualize the democratic project and find that its path is neither straight nor smooth. Many contradictions line the way and negotiations traverse from ideology to identity" (43). Leonardo's review ends up being a rather nice complement to this author's main premise concerning educational outcome: Critical school reform does not only aim to improve student outcomes but also creates the preconditions for broader social emancipation (43).

SYSTEMATIZED FAILURE

Concern with the moral dimensions of education reform (see chapter 8) is no less important in this final chapter which seeks to find some kind of direction for the future so that education reform can stop being the self-aggrandizing activity it has been for far too long. We should all be greatly concerned at the grotesque level of failure of our American public school system. Yet even more horrifying is the knowledge that the school system is reflective of the greater society in which teaching and learning occur. Indeed, these are very unsettling thoughts, but it would be better to resolve our thinking now rather than try to remediate the results of ill-advised and systematically followed reform packages.

The past two decades of failed reforms have left us with children and young adults who can not read with understanding and, worse yet, are morally illiterate. This realization should not surprise us considering the current global instability with its fragile and uncertain peace.

If we want schools to teach peace, we need comprehensive approaches that support the reduction of poverty and social exclusion. In expanding educational opportunities to include the most overlooked groups, we also need to focus on how policies are defined and implemented, by holding policy-makers accountable to children and their parents, particularly to the most impoverished and overlooked groups (Reimers, 2002, 44).

In a utopian world, we might accomplish Reimers's idealized vision:

> It is high time to push aside the corrosive effects of cynicism, moral relativism, and corrupt authoritarianism and go forth in a renewal of the purposes of schools so that they empower all of us to be free, to have equal options in life, and to be able to live in peace with one another. (30)

So then how might we stop grasping for panaceas and begin to "reinvent" schooling so that it fulfills the vision of all well-intentioned people? For sure, in order to do any of this, we must begin by abandoning the strategies that have proven either to not be successful in improving the lives of children or, even more disconcerting, to contribute to the worsening of both teaching and learning and the quality of life for everyone. As Mike Schmoker comments pointedly: "There are straightforward proven means for enhancing achievement in virtually any school. But school improvement planning, like its sister, school reform, too often merely distracts us from our real task: the hard work of improving teaching" (2003, 39). The great organizational theorist Michael Fullan has shown us many times that strategic planning or other similar kinds of plans fail because of the complexity of these plans or because they fail to communicate succinctly with teachers who must implement them (Fullan, 1993). Schmoker reports, after reading hundreds of strategic plans from around the country, that almost none of the plans incorporate simple effective structures into the document, but rather they rely on sections and categories such as "goals," "action plans," "objectives," "timelines," "resources needed," "evaluations," "target areas," and so forth (39). He states that "behind the graphic elegance, and the best intentions, lies a bankrupt model awaiting slow discovery. The first casualty is clarity. The key terms themselves—goals, action steps, evaluations (etc.)—get confused. They wind up being used almost interchangeably. This accounts for a phenomenon that dooms real improvement from the start: for all the planning, many teachers can't remember what their goals are" (39).

And the business community would seem to agree that these plans are more political than effective. Schmoker informs the reader in the same article that the two widely published organizational thinkers James Kouzes and Barry Posner report that the research demonstrates that "Strategic planning doesn't work" (39).

An even broader view of the failings of education reform is offered by the two highly prolific educational theorists John Goodlad and Theodore Sizer (2003). Both researchers have frequently bemoaned the fact that education reform has been misguided and ineffective. Specifically, Goodlad states in an article in which he assesses the "Nation at Risk" report of 1983 that "While we have been narrowing the scope of academic learning, cognitive psychologists have been telling us that the transfer of learning across contexts is quite limited. To assume that high test scores on school subjects predicts such desirable personal and social attributes as civility, decency, civic-mindedness, honesty, dependability, compassion, creativity, and even good work habits is folly. For corporate employers to count on test scores to predict the qualities they want in their employees is an exercise in futility" (2003, 25). He goes on to state emphatically that nationwide implementation of the federal No Child Left Behind Act of 2001 will not give us the schools we need (25).

And Sizer reminds us that the sociologist James Coleman of the University of Chicago chaired a panel that produced a large scholarly volume entitled *Youth: Transition to Adulthood,* in which he explains that every generation has lengthened the amount of schooling for adolescents and that a thoughtful person needs to ask whether society can conceive of no other way for youth to come into adulthood. Furthermore, Coleman points out in the preface to the report that "If schooling were a complete environment then it would, of course, be a good idea for youth to spend a lot of time there" (cited in Sizer and Goodlad, 2003, 24). As Sizer points out all too well, the "Nation at Risk" report needed Coleman's report *Youth* in order to be a complete picture of how we might begin to improve schooling in America.

TOWARD MULTIPLE PERSPECTIVES

Some interesting research was carried out and reported in the AERA publication *Educational Researcher*. In her article (1998) theorist Anna Sfard illustrates a key difference in what she calls "metaphorical mappings," namely that there are two distinctly different ways to look at teaching and learning. One is the acquisition metaphor and the other, the participation metaphor. She notes that the acquisition metaphor has guided research on learning for the past sixty years. Piaget, Vygotsky, and others talk about human behavior vis-à-vis learning in terms of acquiring some pieces of knowledge that were not previously in the individual's mind. Key words in this framework are *knowledge, concept, idea, notion, misconception, sense, schemer, fact, material, contents*. Identity, then, is defined in terms of possession (of knowledge). We have seen the pluses and minuses of this kind of approach illustrated in the previous chapters on curriculum, instruction, and assessment. While there is nothing inherently bad about this kind of metaphor, we have seen its limitations.

In contrast, the participation metaphor has only appeared in the literature since the 1990s. Representing a significant ontological shift, this metaphor alters the focus to the evolving bonds between the individual and others. Identity is defined in terms of the individual becoming part of a greater entity. Key words in this new paradigm are *communication* and *discourse*.

Sfard's distinction between these two kinds of metaphors is significant for us in our discussions of multiple perspectives because it allows a highly differentiated way of looking at teaching and learning. No one can deny the extraordinary contributions of psychologists such as Piaget and Vygotsky; however, *the limitations of psychology have been well established in previous chapters, and it is high time that we allow other kinds of thinking (economics, political science, philosophy, and so forth) so that we might enrich the possibilities of creating a truly effective and life-supporting system of schooling for children.* In contrast to the restricted kind of thinking inherent in strategic planning, Sfard's participation metaphor allows us to view the goal of learning as community building and knowledge as a vehicle toward improved discourse, belonging, participating, and communicating with others. These views are indeed radically different from the traditional psychology-based notions that encourage us to view the goal of learning as individual enrichment and knowledge as a possession. Indeed, this author would have to concur with those who believe that there is something deeply distortive about any conception of human intellect that attempts to divorce cognitive ability from human, social, and affective capacities (in the manner, for example, of an IQ test) (Carr, 2003).

To sum up this author's views on multiple perspectives, let us remind ourselves that the vast majority of curriculum, instruction, and assessment products are based on theories in the field of psychology. We need to open up the whole development of teaching and learning to include, as I have stated previously, fields such as economics, sociology, political science, philosophy, and any others that will accomplish a truly comprehensive view of what teaching and learning might become in order to improve the human condition.

ETIOLOGY OF MEDIOCRE PROGRAMS

Several researchers (Borman et al., 2003) have made an enormous contribution to our understanding of school reform in the publication of their research entitled "Comprehensive School Reform and Achievement: A Meta-Analysis." They provide a rather useful meta-analysis on the achievement effects of CSR (comprehensive school reform) and also summarize the effects of twenty-nine widely implemented models. While it is beyond the scope of this book to delineate the rather extensive research that Borman et al., have provided on these CSR models, it is nonetheless interesting to consider that only three models in particular demonstrated a combined quantity, quality, and statistical significance of evidence to set them apart (125). (*Author's Note:* It is not the intention of this author to revile any studies or researchers; rather, given the magnitude of problems in education that most people agree are getting worse, it is the belief of this author that we must become more critically oriented in our conclusions about education reform or school reform efforts.) Borman et al., admit that a long-term commitment to research-proven educational reform is needed to establish a strong marketplace of scientifically based CSR models.

The authors point out that many of the CSR models are replicable and that the expansion of use of these kinds of models has been fueled by movements such as *systemic- and standards-based reform*, the establishment of the New American Schools Development Corporation, new federal legislation allowing the use of Title 1 funds to support schoolwide educational programs in high poverty schools, and so forth (128). The authors also point out that it is only since the mid-1990s that schoolwide reform has emerged as a prominent strategy for helping to improve the outcomes of at-risk students from high-poverty schools (128). This author mentions the just delineated facts because the CSR models are not only ubiquitous, expanding, growing, and embedding themselves as the "solution" to educational failure but also they have endeared themselves to the public at large; this is a grave problem. The "scale up" of CSR designs is happening at an unprecedented rate such that a growing number of externally developed school reform designs (for example, Accelerated Schools, Core Knowledge, High Schools That Work, Success for All) are being implemented in thousands of schools and serving millions of students throughout the United States (126). The good news is that these externally developed designs provide a model for whole school change. (This author has consulted on whole school change and assessment and concurs that this approach is preferable to heavily and exclusively learner-based strategies.) The bad news is that these programs fail to incorporate broad societal issues in any direct way within the curriculum and fail to address the enormous macrolevel challenges that are global in nature and with which the local environment must contend in order to be successful in the twenty-first century. Be that as it may, CSR models are expanding rapidly, because they have established development and dissemination infrastructures for replicating and supporting implementations across numerous schools (128). Therefore, developers of these programs can transport their models to virtually any school and conduct training on the implementation and evaluation of the model. When the model is very specific, specialized training is required and provided by the developers (128). (This author would be the first to applaud all of the programs in all schools if they were to demonstrate an improvement of the human condition and a lessening of human suffering.)

As mentioned above, the twenty-nine studies that are extensively reviewed in "Comprehensive School Reform and Achievement" do not all enjoy resounding approval from the researchers in terms of the models' ability to meet a combination of high quality, quantity, and statistical significance. Nonetheless, the researchers acknowledge that three models in particular met high standards of accountability. It should be of no surprise to the reader that this author would deem that three out of twenty-nine is, of course, far too few to meet a standard that should be met by any and all school programs. That said, the three programs that did meet high standards were the following: Direct Instruction, School Development Program, and Success for All. This author is familiar with these programs and has observed that the prescriptive nature of all of them does prevent a full, enriched environment of teaching and learning. The researchers acknowledge in their conclusion that others have argued that the dominant perspectives on evaluation and improvement in education suggest that the context of each district, school, and classroom is so distinctive that only highly specific change strategies *mapped to site-specific circumstances* are likely to modify and improve their central functions (169). They go on to say that some CSR models they researched provide a contrast to this opposing point of view. This author would argue that the limitations of any and all CSR models reside in the fact that the evaluation of the success of the models is limited to a psychometric assessment that, by its very definition, can only provide an analysis based on statistics and that compares one set of data to some other set of data.

The three so-called high standard programs, namely Direct Instruction, School Development Program, and Success for All, have some positive features and characteristics that make them tempting to implement in high-poverty, low-achieving school districts. The tendency to implement CSR models in high-risk districts is a natural one and cannot be refuted by this author, except to note once again that these programs do not fulfill a much broader vision of what schooling ought to be. Having said this, the three programs contain narrative summaries, provided by the researchers, which delineate the studies used to describe the effectiveness of each. For example, the research base for each of the three CSR model programs is described as "very extensive and of very good quality" (187, 204, 206). There were not, in any of the cases, any statements by the researchers that any of the CSR models produced effects such as the improved ability to read on the part of the majority of students undergoing the treatment (that is, the program); the improved capacity to deal with social change; or the improved willingness to be more compassionate when confronting human suffering; (or, perhaps, the capacity to address any issue outlined in the 1983 "A Nation at Risk" report that accused American education of being "mediocre").

REINVENTION

When this author refers to the prudent use of reinvention, it is not to be construed that I am advocating a production, all over again, of programs exactly as they have been tried in the past. Nor am I advocating the abandonment of praxis in any schooling environment that may have proven to be successful. *Reinvention* in this sense, and for the purposes of this book, means a return to sound ideas that have been forgotten or abandoned (as explained in parts I and II of this book). Put simply, I would want to reinforce Seller and Hannay's idea when they cite Fullan's suggestion:

> An external change agent cannot represent "one more project." To be effective, the dual preoccupation of external reformers should be to focus on the elements of implementation of the program or initiative in question, but to do so in a way that actively and explicitly helps *integrate* the work of the school. Internal capacity building is a coherence-making proposition which cannot be done from the inside acting alone. (Fullan, 1997, 40, cited by W. Seller and L. Hannay, 197, in Bascia and Hargreaves, 2000)

As complex as education reform is, it is tightly aligned to educational change strategies that are usually grounded in change theory (TQM and other business models). It is not the author's intention to explore which change agents and/or models are best suited to a prudent use of reinvention with an eye toward large-scale improvements in schooling. For example, the CSR discussed above, Success for All, is a good example of one that shows up to be hopeful in terms of research result but falls short of providing the kind of extensive, long-lasting result in terms of changing the very nature of schooling, let alone beginning to affect broader issues of quality of life or human suffering.

MULTIPLE PERSPECTIVES, STANDARDS, AND EXTERNAL FORCES

The final analysis of whether anyone can hope to achieve the kind of grandiose accomplishment that this author is suggesting, namely the improvement of the human condition and the reduction of human suffering, is nonetheless what many hope to achieve by succeeding in an education reform agenda. Now this is of course no easy task, but it is the goal and the vision for what all of us want to create in the future. We have to continue to pursue multiple perspectives that contribute to a rich blending of ideas. As we saw in chapter 8, there is no easy way to pin down the improvement of schooling to a mere program in one or two schools. This kind of an approach, as we have seen, is always doomed to failure since it does not address the macrolevel issues that invariably impinge on the school and community. What is desirable ends up being the pursuit of approaches such as those advocated by U. Bronfenbrenner (1979); H. Gardner (1991); J. P. Miller (2000); G. Wiggins (1993); W. Glasser (1990) ; G. Land and B. Jarman (1992); and P. Freire (1972). What is important in all of these educational researchers' work is that, *together*, they create an eclectic mix of disciplinary and theoretical underpinnings that force us to consider our practice in schools in light of more lofty thinking, with more focus on the bigger picture and with greater emphasis on the ideas that give rise to praxis. The necessary relationships that exist among ideas are perhaps best understood within Paolo Freire's work where he demonstrates that a necessary relationship exists among the pedagogical, political, and philosophical. He advocates a "problem-posing approach to teaching" that integrates these three relationships. Unless we are able to bring together these multiple perspectives, we will have lost a complete, whole rendition of the teaching and learning process.

CONCLUSION

Finally, there is a need to continue the small steps we have taken in terms of paying attention to the education reform programs that have predated our own efforts in the United States. We talked about the problematic nature of reform in New Zealand in chapter 2, and we have seen in chapter 8 that a cultural study of success leads us to understand better that there is an international, universal thread that may connect our interpretation of success. But we also have seen that success in all cases is indeed bound to some specific context, that is, a culture of a country, an ethnicity, or other. If we fail to pay attention to these other aspects of reform, we may well be doomed to repeat the enormous contradictions that are pointed out in a study that Stephen Gorard and Chris Taylor conducted at Cardiff University School of Social Sciences in Cardiff, Wales. Gorard and Taylor very exquisitely demonstrate the incredible difficulty that resides in any kind of use of statistical design or analysis to make one's case for any change in education (2002). Not only are there issues of comparability in forms used in testing, serious questions about the significance of numerical results emanating from test scores, and other serious internal problems involved in relying on a new program, or education reform effort, to guide us toward a confidence that we need to improve the overall schooling for children, but also there are serious concerns relative to many education reform packages that fail to adequately explain variance against background factors such as socioeconomic status, equal educational opportunity, and so forth. As one example, Gorard and Taylor explain in their study that no matter what the improvements over time, there is no evidence to believe that these have "broken" the well-established link between student background and school outcomes (5–18). In apparent confirmation of this, a study at the Center for Longitudinal Studies in London reported that children from poor families are no more likely to get qualifications than they were twenty years ago (Hackett, 2000, in Gorard and Taylor, 2002). Similar conclusions, but for different reasons and using different methods, have also been drawn in France (Duru-Bellat and Kieffer, 2000, in Gorard and Taylor, 2002). The clear implication of various studies conducted in various countries, all of which attempt to find correlations between some kind of program and some kind of learning outcome, does not inspire the kind of confidence that is required to duplicate and replicate reform programs nationally or internationally. We forgot, and we continue to refuse to remind ourselves, that some variables are much more tightly connected to educational outcome than others. As Gorard and Taylor point out, "We agree with the conclusions of Plewis (1999) that the most effective way to tackle any quality in education is by addressing poverty" (14). And, as far as this author knows, there are no education reform acts that specifically tackle this compelling problem.

CONCLUSION

IF THERE IS ONE IDEA WORTH REPEATING from the introduction, it is the idea that widespread educational failure threatens the very fabric of our existence and the quality of our life in the twenty-first century. This is not a comfortable idea to put forth either at the beginning of a book or at the end. Why do I feel compelled to mention it again? Having put forth my platform for education reform, I realize that I have not offered a tangible solution to educational failure. Rather, what I hope to have accomplished is a description of what education reform is currently and how it might be reconstructed in order to address the more pressing problems that contribute to educational failure.

What has become, I hope, patently clear to the reader is the following: Failure in schools is a problem that must be addressed at the macrolevel, that is, at the very least we must address societal problems in order to begin to eliminate failure in schools. How do we do this? It is clear that we must reform the sociopolitical context in which schools reside. Furthermore, this context is made up of several concerns: political, economic, and cultural, to name the most salient ones.

Since the summer of 2000, this author has been examining all available resources that impact the topic of education reform and has found some initial patterns in the way schools have responded to the pressure of sociopolitical forces that have demanded accountability. All in all, there are four main areas that receive the bulk of attention, both verbal and financial: (1) curriculum; (2) instruction; (3) assessment (evaluation); and (4) personnel. While there is nothing earth shattering in the finding that attention is mostly focused on just four major areas of schooling, it is precisely the fact that these four areas have always been the main recipients of symbolic and financial support that causes this author to question the whole meaning of "education reform" and its effects on the lives of students, teachers, parents, and everyone else affected by the mandates of reform so prevalent over the past decade. For the most part, everyone understands the reasons for a focus on curriculum, instruction, and assessment. The fourth area—personnel—eludes analysis at other than a superficial level, that is, matters of class size, student-teacher ratio, and teacher preparation. However, it is in the relationship to outcome that personnel issues take on mammoth importance:

> If you want to understand the root of the achievement gap, it's the teacher gap that exists between the affluent schools and the less affluent schools. It's scandalous. (Haselkorn, a dean at Lesley University in Cambridge, Massachusetts, 2003, 10)

What Haselkorn is referring to involves the wide chasm between qualified and unqualified teachers in our nation's schools. There is a much more credentialed and experienced teacher force that works in suburbia rather than in urban centers. It would seem that this problem is the "hidden curriculum" of personnel planning and threatens to undermine efforts of reform in the other three areas.

More surprising still is the alarmingly small test result difference, as we saw previously, between states with established standards and accountability and those with virtually no standards and no regulations for certifying teachers. Massachusetts, a high-standards state, records no more than 5% to 6% more of students proficient in math than does Iowa, a low-standards state. The amount of gain, once margin of error is factored, seems to be insignificant and brings to the forefront a reasonable query about the importance of standards or national testing or both.

While it is tempting to claim a conclusive negative ruling on the relative merits of most education reform efforts, and then deem the matter closed, I have not done so for very specific reasons. The enormous amount of time, effort, and money that has been allotted to the attempt to improve schooling over the past decade speaks to a much more serious matter for all to ponder: How have we allowed the ridiculous repetition of education reform acts, plans, and strategies (or whatever else "reform" ends up being called) when the problems around us—economy, crime, housing, health care, foreign policy (quality of life issues generally)—continue to pose enormous unmet challenges? Do we fail to see the connection between our failure at reform and the worsening, over time, of all these problems?

So then, what will it really take to create the conditions for a true reform of American education? In chapters 8 and 9 of this book, I have attempted to paint a picture of success in a cultural context and also to emphasize the importance of multiple perspectives and the prudent use of reinvention. In order to have any chance of moving away from the irrelevance of legislated education reform (in terms of having any effect on the daily lives of teachers and students, never mind on the learning outcomes of schools), we will have to convince stakeholders at all levels of the social system that "curriculum" at the highest level of state government, for example, always means something quite different from the teacher's choice of subject content to be taught to specific children in a daily classroom period, and well it should.

Katherine Goff observes that "mathematics, traditionally viewed as a quantitative science, depends upon the qualitative methods of observation and description to understand chaotic systems" (1998, 33). Linear, narrow-minded, cause-effect, sequential planning and/or delivery may prevent or obviate the very outcomes we had hoped for: a better life, a compassionate citizen, a skilled worker, a good neighbor, among others. We may need to tolerate "messiness" in curriculum, instruction, and assessment in order to attain the sort of gestalt outcome that may satisfy better our need to know the result of schooling, accept it, and be happy with it. Or we can continue to bemoan the fact that our students do not show a particular percentage gain on this or that test, even though we do not know what we wanted or why we were seeking it in the first place.

In essence, education reform, as it is now conceived and legislated, does not deserve our continued support. It is time to invite all well-meaning stakeholders, from all disciplines, and begin to create the educational future that we know is not only possible but also indispensable. We require a future imbued with kindness, compassion, moral integrity, and confidence. In other words, we must demand an educational system that improves the human condition and decreases human suffering.

REFERENCES

Adler, M. (1982). *The Paideia proposal: An educational manifesto*. New York: Macmillan.
Altbach, P. G. (1991). Trends in comparative education. *Comparative Education Review* 35 (3): 491–507.
Apple, M. (1982). *Education and power*. Boston: ARK.
———. (1990). *Ideology and curriculum*. New York: Routledge.
———. (1999). *Power, meaning and identity: Essays in critical education studies*. New York: Peter Lang.
———. (2000). *Official knowledge: Democratic education in a conservative age*. New York: Routledge.
Apple, M., and Beyer, L. (Eds.). (1998). *The curriculum: Problems, politics and possibilities*. Albany: SUNY Press.
Barzun, J. (1991). *Begin here: The forgotten conditions of teaching and learning*. Chicago: University of Chicago Press.
———. (2001). Lecture on the history of education. Delivered at Trinity University, Texas, October 24, 2001.
Bascia, N., and Hargreaves, A. (Eds.). (2000). *The sharp edge of educational change: Teaching, leading, and the realities of reform*. New York: RoutledgeFalmer.
Bernstein, B. (1971). *Class, codes and control: Vol. 1: Theoretical studies towards a sociology of language*. London: Routledge and Kegan Paul.
———. (1975). *Class, codes and control: Vol. 3: Towards a theory of educational transmissions*. London: Routledge and Kegan Paul.
Boli, J., Ramirez, F. O., and Meyer, J. W. (1985). Explaining the origins and expansion of mass education. *Comparative Education Review* 29 (2): 145–170.
Borman, G., Hewes, G., Overman, L., and Brown, S. (2003). Comprehensive school reform and achievement: A meta-analysis. *Review of Educational Research* 73 (2): 125–230.
Bourdieu, P. (1977). Cultural reproduction and social reproduction. In *Power and ideology in education*. Ed. J. Karabel and A. H. Halsey. New York: Oxford University Press.
———. (1991). *Language and symbolic power*. Cambridge, MA: Harvard University Press.
Bowles, S., and Gintis, H. (1976). *Schooling in capitalist America: Educational reform and the contradictions of economic life*. New York: Basic.

Bronfenbrenner, U. (1979). *The ecology of human development.* Cambridge, MA: Harvard University Press.
Bruner, J. (1960). *The process of education.* New York: Random House.
———. (1966). *Toward a theory of instruction.* Cambridge, MA: Harvard University Press.
———. (1996). *The culture of education.* Cambridge, MA: Harvard University Press
Bruner, J., Goodnow, J. J., and Austin, G. A. (1967). *A study of thinking.* New York: Science Editions.
Buzzelli, C. A., and Johnston, B. (2002). *The moral dimensions of teaching: Language, power, and culture in classroom interaction.* New York: RoutledgeFalmer.
Caine, R. N., and Caine, G. (1991). *Making connections: Teaching and the human brain.* Alexandria, VA: Association for Supervision and Curriculum Development.
Carr, D. (2003). *Making sense of education: An introduction to the philosophy and theory of education and teaching.* London: RoutledgeFalmer.
Chomsky, N. (1965). *Aspects of the theory of syntax.* Cambridge, MA: MIT Press.
———. (2000). *Chomsky on miseducation.* Lanham, MD : Rowman and Littlefield.
Chubb, J. E., and Moe, T. M. (1990). *Politics, markets and America's schools.* Washington, D.C.: Brookings Institution Press, 140.
Cisneros, S. (1989). *The House on Mango Street.* New York: Vintage.
Commonwealth of Massachusetts. *Selected general laws, including the Massachusetts Education Reform Act of 1993.* January 1, 1996. Boston: Massachusetts Association of School Committees.
The condition of education. (2002). Washington, D.C.: National Center for Education Statistics, OERI, U.S. Department of Education.
Dewey, J. (1902). *The child and the curriculum.* New York: Macmillan.
———. (1916). *Democracy and education.* New York: Macmillan.
———. (1938). *Experience and education.* New York: Macmillan.
Durkheim, É. (1956). *Education and Sociology.* New York: The Free Press.
Eisner, E. (Ed.). (1985). *Learning and teaching the ways of knowing.* Chicago: University of Chicago Press.
Elkind, D. (1978). *A sympathetic understanding of the child.* Boston: Allyn and Bacon.
———. (1993). *Images of the young child.* Washington, D.C.: National Association for the Education of Young Children.
Evans, R. (2002a). Family matters: The real crisis in education. *Education Week* XXI (37): 37, 48.
———.(2002b). *The human side of school change.* Jossey-Bass.
Fishman, J. (1972). *The Sociology of language: An interdisciplinary social science approach to language in society.* Rowley, MA: Newbury House Publishers.
Fiske, E. B., and Ladd, H.F. (2000). A distant laboratory: Learning cautionary tales from New Zealand schools. *Education Week* XIX (36): 38, 56.
———. (2001). *When schools compete: A cautionary tale.* Washington, D.C.: Brookings Institution Press.
Freire, P. (1972). *Pedagogy of the oppressed.* New York: Penguin.
———. (2000). *Education for critical consciousness.* New York: Continuum International Publishing Group.
Fullan, M. (1993). *Change forces: Probing the depths of educational reform.* Bristol, PA: Falmer Press.
Gagne, R. (1967). Instruction in the conditions of learning. In *Instruction: Some contemporary viewpoints.* Ed. L. Siegel. New York: Harper and Row.

References

Gardner, H. (1983). *Frames of mind: The theory of multiple intelligences.* New York: Basic.
———. (1991). *The unschooled mind: How children think and how schools should teach.* New York: Basic.
Giroux, H. (1980). Reproduction and resistance in classroom pedagogy. In *Social Practice.* Special issue: *The Politics of Education* (Spring) 29–46.
Giroux, H., and Aronowitz, S. (1985). *Education under siege: The conservative, liberal and radical debate over schooling.* South Hadley, MA: Bergin and Garvey.
Glasser, W. (1990). *The quality school.* New York: Harper Collins.
Glatthorn, A. (1991). *Curriculum leadership.* A special handbook created for the Massachusetts Association for Supervision and Curriculum Development.
———. (1995). *School improvement with a curricular focus.* Handbook prepared for the Massachusetts Association for Supervision and Curriculum Development.
Glickman, C. (2000). The good and bad of standards. *Education Update* 42 (4): 7.
Goff, K. (1998). Chaos, collaboration, and curriculum: A deliberative process. *Journal of Curriculum and Supervision* 14 (1): 29–42.
Goodlad, J., and Sizer, T. (2003). Twenty years later. *Education Week* XXII (32): 24–25, 36.
Goodman, K. S. (1967). Reading: A psycholinguistic guessing game. *Journal of the Reading Specialist,* 6, 126–35.
Gorard, S., and Taylor, C. (2002). Market forces and standards in education: A preliminary consideration. *British Journal of Sociology of Education* 23 (1): 5–18.
Gray, J. G. (1968). *The promise of wisdom: An introduction to philosophy of education.* Philadelphia: J. B. Lippincott.
Hart, T. (2001). *From information to transformation: Education for the evolution of consciousness.* New York: Peter Lang.
Haselkorn, D. (2003). In Quality counts. *Education Week* XXII (17): 10.
Hersh, R. H. (2000). Foundations for change. *Education Week* XIX (22): 40, 60.
Hill, H. C. (2001). Policy and not enough: Language and the interpretation of state standards. *American Educational Research Journal* 38 (2): 289–318.
Holton, G. (2003). An insider's view of A Nation at Risk and why it still matters. *The Chronicle of Higher Education* XLIX (33): B13–15.
Hunt, D. E. (1971). *Matching models in education.* Toronto: Ontario Institute for Studies in Education.
Johnson, D. W., and Johnson, R. T. (1974). Instructional goal structure: Cooperative, competitive, or individualistic. *Review of Educational Research* 44: 213–40.
Johnson, D. W., Maruyana, G., Johnson, R. T., Nelson, D., and Skon, L. (1981). Effects of cooperative, competitive, and individualistic goal structures on achievement: A meta-analysis. *Psychological Bulletin* 89 (1): 47–62.
Joyce, B., and Weil, M. (1972). *Models of teaching.* Boston: Allyn and Bacon.
King, E. W. (1999). *Looking into the lives of children: A worldwide view.* Australia: James Nicholas.
Kohn, A. (2000). Standardized testing and its victims: Inconvenient facts and inequitable consequences. *Education Week* XX (4): 46–47, 60.
Labaree, D. (2000). *Lessons of a century.* Bethesda, MD: Editorial Projects in Education.
Land, G., and Jarman, B. (1992). *Breakpoint and beyond: Mastering the future—today.* New York: Harper Collins.
Leech, G. (1974). *Semantics.* Great Britain: Penguin Books.
Leonardo, Z. (2003). The agony of school reform: Race, class, and the elusive search for social justice. Book review. *Educational Researcher* 32 (3): 37–43.

Levine, A. (2001). An endgame for school reform. *Education Week* XXI (15): 52.
Macedo, D. (Ed.). (2000). *Chomsky on miseducation*. Lanham, MD: Rowman and Littlefield, 48.
Manzo, K. K., and Galley, M. (2003). Math climbs, reading flat on '03 NAEP. *Education Week* XXIII (12): 1, 18.
McLaren, P. (1998). *Life in schools: An introduction to critical pedagogy in the foundations of education*. New York: Longman.
Miller, J. P. (2000). *Education and the soul: Toward a spiritual curriculum*. Albany: SUNY Press.
Molnar, A. (Ed.). (1985). *Current thought on curriculum*. Alexandria, VA: Association for Supervision and Curriculum Development.
A nation at risk. (1983). Report by the National Commission on Excellence in Education.
The nation's report card: Mathematics 2000. (2001). Education Commission of the States, Denver, Colorado. Washington, D.C.: National Center for Education Statistics.
Newkirk, T. (2000). A mania for rubrics: Will the standards movement make satire (and good writing) obsolete? *Education Week* XX (2): 41.
Newman, J. (2002). *America's teachers: An introduction to education*. 4th ed. Boston: Allyn and Bacon, 275.
Nieto, S. (2002). *Language, culture, and teaching: Critical perspectives for a new century*. Mahwah, NJ: Lawrence Erlbaum.
No Child Left Behind (NCLB) Law. (2001). PL 107–10, ESEA 02. http://www.nclb.gov.
O'Keefe, J., and Nadel, L. (1978). *The hippocampus as a cognitive map*. Oxford: Clarendon.
Olson, L. (2003). The great divide. *Quality counts*. Bethesda, MD: Editorial Projects in Education.
Perkins, D. (1992). *Smart schools: Better thinking and learning for every child*. New York: The Free Press.
Perrone, V. (Ed.) (1991). *Expanding student assessment*. Alexandria, VA: Association for Supervision and Curriculum Development.
Phillips, G. W. (2002). *The Condition of Education*. Washington, D.C.: U.S. Department of Education.
Popham, W. J. (2001). *The truth about testing*. Alexandria, VA: Association for Supervision and Curriculum Development.
Porter, A., and Chester, M. (2002). Building a high-quality assessment and accountability program: The Philadelphia example. In *Brookings Papers on Education Policy*. Diane Ravitch (Ed.). Washington, D.C.: Brookings Institution Press, 285–337.
Position statement of the American Educational Research Association concerning high-stakes testing in preK–12 education. (2000). *Educational Researcher* 29 (8): 24–25.
Price, H. (2001). The preparation gap: Eliminate it first, then the achievement gap. *Education Week* XXI (13): 34, 48.
Quality counts. (1998). *Education Week* XVII (17): 76–81.
Quality counts. (2003). *Education Week* XXII (17): 62, 80–99.
Ramirez, F.O., and Boli-Bennett, J. (1987). The political construction of mass schooling: European origins and worldwide institutionalization. Paper presented at American Sociological Association meeting, Chicago.
Reich, R. B. (2001). Standards for what? *Education Week* XX (41): 48, 64.
Reimers, F. (2002). War, education, and peace. *Education Week* XXII (15): 30, 44.
Resnick, L. B. (1987). *Education and learning to think*. Washington, D.C.: National Academy Press.

Rich, J. M. (1968). *Education and human values*. Reading, MA: Addison-Wesley.
Roselli, A. M. (2003). Synthesis of research on education reform. Unpublished.
Rothman, R. (1992). Rand study finds serious problems in VT portfolio program. *Education Week* XII (15): 1, 20.
Saphier, J., and Gower, R. (1979). *The skillful teacher*. Carlisle, MA: Research for Better Teaching.
Sarasin, S. (1990). *The predictable failure of educational reform*. San Francisco: Jossey-Bass.
Schmoker, M. (2003). Planning for failure? Too much of schools' improvement planning misses the mark. *Education Week* XXII (22): 39.
Senge, P. (1994). *The fifth discipline: The art and practice of the learning organization*. New York: Doubleday.
Sergiovanni, T. (1995). *The principalship: A reflective practice perspective*. 3rd ed. Boston: Allyn and Bacon.
Sfard, A. (1998). On two metaphors for learning and the dangers of choosing just one. *Educational Researcher* 27 (2): 4–13.
Slavin, R. E. (1983). *Cooperative learning*. New York: Longman.
———. (1990). Mastery learning reconsidered. *Review of Educational Research* 60 (2): 300–302.
Spady, W. (1988). Organizing for results: The basis of authentic restructuring and reform. *Education Leadership* 46 (2): 4–8.
Technology Counts. (2003). *Education Week* XXII (35): 58–59.
Thompson, K. (2002). *Émile Durkheim*. Rev. ed. London: Routledge.
Trifonas, P. P. (Ed.). (2000). *Revolutionary pedagogies: Cultural politics, instituting education, and the discourse of theory*. New York: RoutledgeFalmer.
Tyler, R. W. (1949). *Basic principles of curriculum and instruction*. Chicago: University of Chicago Press.
Viadero, D. (2001). Whole-school projects show mixed results. *Education Week* XX (10): 24–25.
Vygotsky, L. S. (1962). *Thought and language*. Cambridge, MA: MIT Press.
———. (1978). *Mind in society: The development of higher psychological processes*. Cambridge, MA: Harvard University Press.
Webster's thesaurus. (1994). New York: PMC.
Weinstein, D. (1987). *Curriculum mapping for administrators*. Englewood Cliffs, NJ: Prentice Hall.
Wiggins, G. (1993). *Assessing student performance: Exploring the purpose and limits of testing*. San Francisco: Jossey-Bass.
Wiggins, G., and McTighe, J. (1998). *Understanding by design*. Alexandria, VA: Association for Supervision and Curriculum Development.
Wilber, K. (1995). *Sex, ecology, spirituality: The spirit of evolution*. Boston: Shambhala.
Wolf, D. P. (1990). Assessment as an episode of learning. Paper presented at the conference on Constructed Response, Princeton, NJ, Educational Testing Service, November 30–December 1, 1990.

INDEX

A

accidental knowledge, 79–80, 84
achievement, unfulfilled expectations of, 16, 148
Adler, M., 89
advance organizer, 93–94
AERA (American Educational Research Association), 49–51
Altbach, P. G., 124
anomie, 126
Apple, M., 56, 67, 84, 104, 134
Aronowitz, S., 84
ASCD (Association for Supervision and Curriculum Development), 73
assessment as art, 105
assessment, 103–106
Ausubul, D., 93–94
authenticity, 115–116
AYP (adequate yearly progress), 19–20

B

Barzun, J., 68–69, 100–101
Bascia, N., 133
Bell, T.H., 17
Bernstein, B., 125, 127–128, 134
Boli, J., 124
Boli-Bennett, J., 124
Borman, G., 141
Bourdieu, P., 69, 129
Bowles, S., 84
Bronfenbrenner, U., 144

Bruner, J., 65, 88–89
Bush, G. W., 19
Buzzelli, C. A., 129–131

C

Caine, G., 98–99
Caine, R., 98–99
Carr, D., 141
change theory, 46–47, 144–145
Chester, M.,
Chomsky, N., 61, 66–67
Chubb, J. E., 49
Cisneros, S., 130
Coleman, J., 139–140
concept attainment, 95–96
contextual issues in assessment, 116–118
cooperative learning, 94–95
CSR (comprehensive school reform), 142
cultural identity, 131
cultural reproduction, 124–125
curriculum design, 75–77

D

Davis, P., 23
Dewey, J., 89
Durkheim, E., 125–127

E

Education Commission of the States, 7

education reform, 1, 63–65, 147–149
educational failure, 147
Eisner, E., 89
Elkind, D., 89
equal educational opportunity, 145
Evans, R., 51–52

F

family, 52
Fishman, J., 69
Fiske, E. B., 36
Freire, P., 84, 89, 124, 144–145
Fullan, M., 139, 143–144
fundamental knowledge, 79–80, 82–83

G

Gagne, R., 89
Galley, M., 8
Gardner, H., 84, 89, 144
gestalt, 149
Gintis, H., 84
Giroux, H., 84, 104
Glasser, W., 144
Glatthorn, A., 82, 85, 97–98
Glickman, C., 26–27, 29
Goff, K., 149
Goodlad, J., 139
Goodman, K., 97
Gorard, S., 145–146
Gower, R., 90
Gray, J. G., 84

H

habit, 114–115
Hargreaves, A., 133
Hart, T., 81–82, 84
Haselkorn, D., 148
Hersh, R. H., 30
high-stakes testing, 49–51
Hill, H. C., 57
Holton, G., 18

J

Jarman, B., 144
Johnston, B., 129–131
Joyce, B., 89, 92

K

King, E. W., 124
Kohn, A., 41–43
Kouzes, J., 139

L

Laboree, D., 45
Ladd, H. F., 36
Land, G., 144
Leech, J., 61
Leonardo, Z., 136–138
Levine, A., 52–53
linguistics in action, 57–60

M

MA Education Reform Act of 1993, 23–26, 30–36
Manzo, K., 8
MCAS testing, 27–29, 44–45
McLaren, P., 104, 134
McTigue, J., 107
metaphorical mappings, 140
Meyer, J. W., 124
Miller, J., 85, 144
models of teaching, 92–96
Moe, T. M., 49
Molnar, A., 73–74
moral judgment, 132
morphology, 58–59
multiple perspectives, 141, 149

N

Nadel, L., 99
NAEP scores/analysis, 8–15, 44–45
Nation at Risk, A, 3, 17–18
National Center for Education Statistics, 8
Nation's Report Card, The, 8
NCLB (No Child Left Behind) legislation, 3, 19–20
Newkirk, T., 29–30
Newman, J., 78
Nieto, S., 131

O

O'Keefe, J., 99

Index

P

Perrone, V., 104–105
Phillips, G. W., 18, 45–46
phonology, 59–60
Piaget, J., 66–67, 140
policy, 58
Popham, W. J., 116–118
Porter, A., 119
portfolios, 112–114
Posner, B., 139
poverty, 46, 146
praxis, 145
Price, H., 47–48
problem-posing approach, 145
psycholinguistic model, 64

Q

Quality Counts, 15
quality of life, 148

R

Ramirez, F. O., 124
Reagan, R., 17
reconceptualization of reform, 67–69
Reich, R. B., 43
Reimers, F., 138
reinvention, 143–144, 149
Rich, J. M., 133
Rothman, R., 112

S

Saphier, J., 90
Sapir-Whorfian hypothesis, 70
Sarasin, S., 56
Schmoker, M., 138–139
SEM (standard error of measurement), 46
semantics, 60–61
Senge, P., 56
Sergiovanni, T., 56
SES (socioeconomic status), 117, 129
Sfard, A., 140
site-specific reform, 143
Sizer, T., 139
sociology of education, 124
sociopolitical context, 147
Spady, W., 82

standards, 148
strategic planning, 139
success, 148–149
syntax, 60
systematized failure, 138

T

Taylor, C., 145–146
Technology Counts, 16–17
technology, 16–17
Thompson, K., 125–126
Trifonas, P., 2
Tyler, R., 89

V

Vygotsky, L., 65–66, 131, 140

W

Weil, M., 89, 92
Weinstein, D., 74
whole school reform, 2
wholistic assessment, 107–111
Wiggins, G., 107, 114–116, 144
Wilbur, K., 81
Wolf, D. P., 111–113

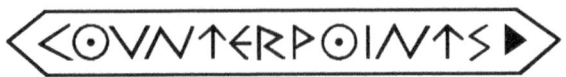

Studies in the Postmodern Theory of Education

General Editor
Shirley R. Steinberg

Counterpoints publishes the most compelling and imaginative books being written in education today. Grounded on the theoretical advances in criticalism, feminism, and postmodernism in the last two decades of the twentieth century, Counterpoints engages the meaning of these innovations in various forms of educational expression. Committed to the proposition that theoretical literature should be accessible to a variety of audiences, the series insists that its authors avoid esoteric and jargonistic languages that transform educational scholarship into an elite discourse for the initiated. Scholarly work matters only to the degree it affects consciousness and practice at multiple sites. Counterpoints' editorial policy is based on these principles and the ability of scholars to break new ground, to open new conversations, to go where educators have never gone before.

For additional information about this series or for the submission of manuscripts, please contact:

> Shirley R. Steinberg
> c/o Peter Lang Publishing, Inc.
> 29 Broadway, 18th floor
> New York, New York 10006

To order other books in this series, please contact our Customer Service Department:
> (800) 770-LANG (within the U.S.)
> (212) 647-7706 (outside the U.S.)
> (212) 647-7707 FAX

Or browse online by series:
> www.peterlang.com